CW01574565

MEDITERRANEAN DIET COOKBOOK

FOR BEGINNERS

Copyright

MEDITERRANEAN DIET COOKBOOK

FOR BEGINNERS

Discover The Flavors of the Mediterranean with **2000 Days** of Simple, Delicious and Quick Recipes, Plus a **60-Day Meal Plan for Healthy Weight Loss**

ANNA J. COOK

Dedication

To my dedicated collaborators and beloved family,

This book is a testament to the power of collaboration, support, and love. Without your unwavering belief in this project, it would not have come to fruition. Thank you for being the driving force behind these pages and for sharing your expertise, creativity, and passion.

To my collaborators, your commitment to culinary excellence and attention to detail have brought these recipes to life. Your tireless efforts in testing, refining, and perfecting each dish have ensured that this cookbook is a true reflection of the vibrant flavors and wholesome nature of Mediterranean cuisine.

To my family, you have been my rock throughout this journey. Your unwavering support, encouragement, and patience have fueled my passion and inspired me to explore the depths of Mediterranean cooking. Thank you for sharing countless meals, for your honest feedback, and for being my most trusted taste-testers.

May this book be a celebration of our shared love for good food, good health, and good company. May the recipes within these pages bring warmth to your kitchens, joy to your tables, and nourishment to your bodies. May they serve as a reminder of the memories we have created together and the traditions we hold dear.

To my collaborators and family, I am forever grateful for your contributions and unwavering support. This book is as much yours as it is mine, and I am honored to have embarked on this culinary journey with each and every one of you.

With heartfelt appreciation,

About the author

Anna J. Cook is a highly accomplished female writer and culinary enthusiast, celebrated for her expertise in the Mediterranean diet and her passion for sharing its culinary wonders with the world. With a deep-rooted love for wholesome, flavorful food, she has become a leading voice in promoting the Mediterranean lifestyle as a pathway to optimal health and well-being.

Hailing from a culturally diverse background, **Anna J. Cook** was raised with a deep appreciation for the vibrant flavors and traditions of Mediterranean cuisine. Drawing upon her rich heritage and her own culinary explorations, she embarked on a mission to create a cookbook that would capture the essence of this iconic way of eating.

Her book, is a culinary masterpiece that showcases the diversity and beauty of Mediterranean flavors. Through meticulous research, extensive travels, and countless hours spent experimenting in the kitchen, **Anna J. Cook** has curated a collection of recipes that not only nourish the body but also ignite the senses.

With each page, **Anna J. Cook** transports readers to the sun-kissed shores of the Mediterranean, guiding them on a gastronomic journey that celebrates the region's abundance of fresh produce, aromatic herbs, and heart-healthy ingredients. Her cookbook is a testament to the notion that healthy eating need not be a sacrifice, but rather a delightful and fulfilling experience.

Beyond the recipes themselves, **Anna J. Cook** infuses her cookbook with cultural insights and practical tips for incorporating the Mediterranean diet into everyday life. She empowers readers to embrace this way of eating as a sustainable lifestyle choice, encouraging them to find joy in preparing wholesome meals and savoring the nourishing flavors that abound in Mediterranean cuisine.

With her cookbook as a guiding light, **Anna J. Cook** continues to empower people to embrace the Mediterranean lifestyle, savor every bite, and nourish their bodies with the wholesome and delectable flavors that define this iconic way of eating. Through her words and recipes, she invites readers to discover the joy and vitality that come from embracing the Mediterranean diet and cultivating a lifelong love affair with nourishing food.

TABLE OF CONTENTS

INTRODUCTION

Welcome to "The Mediterranean Diet Cookbook for Beginners 2023". This is not just a cookbook; rather, it is an invitation to embark on a tasty journey with the area of the Mediterranean and investigate its illustrious history. It's a passport to better health and an improved lifestyle, all designed to inspire, instruct, and encourage you on your journey to a healthier you.

First and foremost, let's understand what the Mediterranean Diet is. The eating habits and way of life of people living in various countries surrounding the Mediterranean Sea, such as Italy, Greece, Spain, and Morocco, are the foundation of the Mediterranean diet. It not's only the food but also about a holistic approach to a healthier and stronger lifestyle, including regular physical activity and an emphasis on sharing meals as well as recipes qualities with family and friends. This diet put its aims on the wide range of fresh, whole foods, some healthy fats like olive, avocado or coconut oil, veggies, legumes, nuts, fresh fruits, whole grains, and seeds. Red meat isn't as popular as fish and chicken; red wine is taken only in small amounts.

One of the standout features of the Mediterranean diet is its extensive health benefits. Researchers have discovered that it reduces the risk of various chronic diseases, including cardiovascular

disease, cancer, diabetes, and Alzheimer's. This is mostly because the diet put the aims on heart-healthy monounsaturated fats, lean proteins of red meat, fresh fruits, fresh veggies, and legumes that are high in fiber, and it limits the number of processed foods people eat.

The Mediterranean diet is also highly praised for being easy to follow. It's not about restrictive rules or cutting out entire food groups. Instead, it's about making decisions that are better for your health, eating a wide variety of foods while maintaining moderation, and preparing nutritious and delicious meals. This cookbook provides you with a bundle of recipes and ideas for main courses that will make following the Mediterranean diet less complicated, more satisfying, and more pleasurable.

We understand that change, especially regarding dietary habits, is often easier said than done. As a result, you can think of this book as a companion, a guide, and a resource that will assist you in navigating this transition at your own pace. The purpose of this cookbook is to investigate the applicability of Mediterranean cuisine and to uncover the ways in which its guidelines can be incorporated into your day-to-day life, regardless of where you happen to call home.

So, let's embark on this exciting journey towards a healthier, happier lifestyle - one delicious meal at a time. Enjoy exploring the Mediterranean way of life through its food, the simplicity of its preparation, and the celebration of its vibrant flavors.
Welcome aboard, and bon appétit!

Chapter 1: The Food Pyramid of the Mediterranean Diet

The Mediterranean Diet, often hailed as one of the healthiest diets globally, has garnered much praise and attention. While the diet is primarily about the foods you eat, it's also about the lifestyle accompanying it - one that emphasizes physical activity, moderation, and enjoyment of meals as a communal event.

At the heart of the Mediterranean Diet is its food pyramid. This pyramid is a guiding tool, offering a visual representation of the diet's principles and providing an understanding of the foods (and their portions) that may form the foundation of your diet.

What to Eat

Embrace the core of the Mediterranean Diet with these food groups. They form the heart of the cuisine, offering the nutrients and flavors that define this celebrated way of eating. Fresh fruits, a lot of fresh vegetables, whole grains, legumes, lean proteins of red meat (beef or lamb), and heart-healthy fats looks in the Mediterranean diet. Explore these categories and their examples to get started on your journey.

Food Group	Sub-Category	Examples
Fruits	Berries, Citrus Fruits, Pome Fruits, Melons, Tropical Fruits	Strawberries, Oranges, Apples, Watermelon, Bananas
Vegetables	Leafy Greens, Cruciferous Vegetables, Root Vegetables, Squash	Spinach, Broccoli, Carrots, Zucchini
Whole Grains	Cereals, Bread, Pasta	Whole grain bread, Whole grain pasta, Oats
Legumes	Beans, Peas, Lentils	Chickpeas, Green peas, Red lentils
Nuts and Seeds	Tree Nuts, Ground Nuts, Seeds	Almonds, Peanuts, Flaxseeds
Healthy Fats	Oils, Whole Food Fats	Extra-virgin olive oil, Avocados
Fish and Seafood	Fatty Fish, Shellfish	Salmon, Shrimp
Poultry	Chicken, Turkey	Skinless chicken breast, Turkey slices
Dairy	Cheese, Yogurt	Feta cheese, Greek yogurt
Herbs and Spices	Fresh Herbs, Dried Herbs, Spices	Basil, Dried oregano, Cinnamon
Wine	Red Wine, White Wine	A glass of red or white wine

What to Eat Occasionally

This section is all about balance. The Mediterranean diet understands that variety is the spice of life. Hence, while not consumed daily, some food groups have their place in this dietary plan. Red meats, eggs, and natural sweeteners are foods to enjoy moderately and infrequently. This practice ensures a wide array of nutrients while maintaining balance and heart health.

Food Group	Sub-Category	Examples
Eggs	Hen's Eggs, Other Eggs	Chicken eggs, Duck eggs
Red Meats	Beef, Pork, Lamb	Lean cuts of beef, Pork tenderloin, Lamb chops
Sweeteners	Natural Sweeteners	Honey, Maple syrup
Processed Poultry	Sausages, Cold Cuts	Chicken sausages, Turkey slices

What to Avoid

For every 'yes' in a diet, there's usually a 'no,' and it's no different in the Mediterranean Diet. But think of these less as prohibitions and more as swaps. Instead of refined grains, go for whole ones. Instead of sugary drinks, why not water with a squeeze of fresh lemon? By minimizing the intake of these food items, you're saying 'yes' to healthier alternatives, better nutrition, and more authentic flavors. Let's explore the food categories the Mediterranean diet advises us to avoid for a healthier lifestyle.

Food Group	Sub-Category	Examples
Refined Grains	Bread, Pasta, Rice	White bread, White pasta, White rice
Processed Foods	Fast Foods, Sweet Snacks, Savory Snacks	Fast food burgers, Cookies, Potato chips
Sugary Drinks	Carbonated Drinks, Sweetened Coffee, and Tea	Soda, Sweetened iced tea
Refined Oils	Cooking Oils, Salad Oils	Canola oil, Soybean oil
Trans Fats	Margarine, Fried Foods, Packaged Foods	Stick margarine, Fried chicken, Store-bought cakes, and cookies

With this guide in mind, you're well on your way to understanding the Mediterranean diet's structure. The following chapters will dive deeper into each component of this diet, provide a more detailed food list, and offer tips on incorporating these principles into your everyday life.

Remember, the Mediterranean diet is not about deprivation. It's about a diverse, balanced consumption of nutrient-rich foods nourishing your body and palate with healthy physical activity and social connection. So, as you move forward in this journey, embrace the diet's spirit - one of balance, variety, and enjoyment.

Chapter 2: The Principles of Mediterranean Cuisine

Mediterranean cuisine is a symphony of flavors and textures, drawing on a rich tapestry of cultural influences. Its foundations rest upon three pillars: the importance of olive oil, the use of distinct aromas and spices, and the preparation of raw dishes. These principles are not merely guidelines for cooking; they are a testament to the region's history, traditions, and the Mediterranean way of life.

The Importance of Olive Oil

Olive oil, well known as "liquid gold," is a crucial element of the cuisine of the Mediterranean. Olive oil is more than just an ingredient; it is the lifeblood of Mediterranean cuisine, playing as a cooking medium, flavor enhancer, and food preservative. Olive oil is one of the suspicious components of Mediterranean cuisine.

The first olives were cold pressed without heat or chemicals, producing extra virgin olive oil, the finest quality olive oil with the richest flavor. It has a distinct fruity flavor that lends dishes a sense of depth and richness, whether used for sautéing, frying, or as a finishing drizzle on a completed dish.

Beyond its culinary uses, olive oil also has numerous health benefits. It's rich in monounsaturated fatty acids, which can help lower harmful cholesterol levels and improve heart health. Olive oil is also loaded with antioxidants, which can combat inflammation and help protect the body from cellular damage.

In the Mediterranean diet, olive oil replaces butter and other unhealthy fats, making it a healthier choice for everyday cooking and baking. Its versatile nature makes it perfect for creating diverse dishes, from simple salads to complex main courses.

Typical Aromas and Spices

Mediterranean cooking is all about spices and herbs. They bring dishes to life, adding complexity, depth, and a unique sense of place to every meal. Herbs like basil, parsley, rosemary, oregano, and thyme frequently provide fresh, vibrant flavors that elevate dishes.

In addition, spices are an important factor. Cinnamon, paprika powder, saffron thirds, cumin seeds, and coriander leaves/seeds are just a few examples of different spices. These spices add warmth, heat, sweetness, and a depth of flavor that can transform even the simplest dish into something truly special.

Garlic is another staple, often used in marinades, dressings, sauces, and as a base flavor for many dishes. Lemons are also used extensively, adding a bright, citrusy note that balances the flavors and adds a refreshing touch.

The use of herbs, spices, and other aromatics in Mediterranean cuisine highlights an important diet principle - flavor doesn't need to come from unhealthy sources like saturated fats or processed foods. Instead, you can create mouthwatering, satisfying meals using natural, healthful ingredients.

The Preparation of Raw Dishes

Mediterranean cuisine has a profound respect for ingredients' natural flavors, which is beautifully showcased in its raw dishes. Fresh, high-quality produce, lightly seasoned and minimally processed, allows each ingredient's inherent flavors to shine through.

A prime illustration of this is the authentic Greek salad, which typically consists of ripe tomatoes, cucumbers, ripe olives, red onion, and feta cheese, all beaten with olive oil, vinegar, and various spices. This dish's simplicity highlights the freshness of its ingredients and the flavor harmony that can be accomplished with minimal effort.

Another excellent example is crudo, a dish often found in Italian coastal regions, where thinly sliced raw fish or seafood is dressed with olive oil, lemon juice, and seasonings.

Carpaccio, a traditional Italian dish of thinly sliced raw meat or fish dressed with olive oil, lemon juice, and capers, is another testament to the Mediterranean cuisine's knack for preparing raw dishes.

These raw dishes underscore the importance of fresh, high-quality ingredients in the Mediterranean diet. The focus is on preserving the food's natural flavors and nutritional value rather than transforming or masking them through heavy cooking or processing.

In conclusion, the principles of Mediterranean cuisine - the prominent use of olive oil, the rich array of herbs and spices, and the preparation of raw dishes - are key to understanding the diet's appeal and health benefits. By embracing these principles, you're not only adopting a healthier way of eating but also immersing yourself in a rich, vibrant culinary tradition that celebrates the simple joy of eating well.

MEASUREMENT CONVERSIONS

Volume Equivalents (Liquid)

Standard	US Standard (Ounces)	Metric (Approximate)
2 Tablespoons	1 fl. oz	30 ml
¼ cup	2 fl. oz	60 ml
½ cup	4 fl. oz	120 ml
1 cup	8 fl. oz	240 ml
1½ cup	12 fl. oz	366 ml
2 cups or 1 pint	16 fl. oz	476 ml
4 cups or 1 quart	32 fl. oz	1 L
1 gallon	128 fl. oz	4 L

Oven Tempratures

Fahrenheit (F)	Celsius (c) (Approximate)
250 °F	120°C
300°F	150°C
325°F	165°C
350°F	180°C
375°F	190°C
400°F	200°C
425°F	220°C
450°F	230°C

Volume Equivalents (Dry)

Standard	Metric (Approximate)
⅛ teaspoon	0.5 ml
¼ teaspoon	1 ml
½ teaspoon	2 ml
¾ teaspoon	4 ml
1 teaspoon	5 ml
1 tablespoon	15 ml
¼ cup	59 ml
⅓ cup	79 ml
½ cup	118 ml
⅔ cup	156 ml
¾ cup	177 ml
1 cup	235 ml
2 cups of 1 pint	475 ml
3 cups	700 ml
4 cups or 1 quart	1 L

Weight equiavalents

Standard	Metric (Approximate)
½ Ounce	15 g
1 Ounce	30 g
2 Ounce	60 g
4 Ounce	115 g
8 Ounce	225 g
12 Ounce	340 g
16 Ounce or 1 pound	455 g

Chapter 3:

20 Mediterranean Breakfast Recipe

QUINOA BREAKFAST BOWL WITH BERRIES AND NUTS

Ingredients

- 1/2 cup raw quinoa
- 1 cup water
- 1 cup mixed berries
- 2 tablespoons chopped nuts (almonds, walnuts, etc.)
- Honey or maple syrup, to taste

Directions

1. Rinse the quinoa under water until it runs clear.
2. In a saucepan, add water to a boil. Add the quinoa and reduce heat to low, cover, and simmer for 13-15 minutes until all water is absorbed.
3. Once the quinoa is cooked, divide it into two bowls.
4. Top each bowl with a half cup of mixed berries, one tablespoon of chopped nuts, and sweeten with honey/maple syrup to taste.

Nutritions

320 calories, 12g Fat, 10g Protein, 45g Carbohydrate per serving

PREPARATION TIME: 5 MIN

COOKING TIME: 15 MIN

SERVINGS: 2

VEGGIE AND WHOLE GRAIN SCRAMBLE

Ingredients

- 4 eggs
- 1/2 cup cooked whole grains (quinoa, farro, or bulgur)
- 1/2 cup chopped vegetables (tomatoes, bell peppers, onions)
- 2 tablespoons feta cheese
- Salt and pepper, to taste
- 1 tablespoon olive oil

Directions

1. Put the non-stick frying pan over medium heat, warm the olive oil.
2. Add the finely chopped vegetables and
3. cook them till tender.
4. Beat the eggs in a bowl, then add the cooked whole grains.
5. In the frying pan with the veggies, add the egg mixture. Cook while continuously stirring until the eggs are set.
6. Season with salt and pepper and sprinkle with feta cheese before serving

Nutritions

260 calories, 12g Fat, 16g Protein, 26g Carbohydrate per serving

PREPARATION TIME: 10 MIN

COOKING TIME: 10 MIN

SERVINGS: 2

BUCKWHEAT PANCAKES WITH FRESH BERRIES

Ingredients

- 1 cup buckwheat flour
- 1½ cups almond milk
- 1 tablespoon honey
- 1 egg
- 1 teaspoon baking powder
- Pinch of salt
- 1 cup fresh berries

Directions

1. Mix the buckwheat flour, baking powder, and salt in a bowl. Whisk together the almond milk, egg, and honey in another bowl.
2. Blend the dry components into the wet ingredients gradually. Lightly lubricate a non-stick frying pan and heat it over medium heat.
3. For each pancake, pour 1/4 cup of batter onto the pan. Cook until surface bubbles appear, then turn the food over and continue cooking until the other side is browned.
4. Serve with fresh berries.

Nutritions

275 calories, 6g Fat, 10g Protein, 50g Carbohydrate per serving

PREPARATION TIME: 10 MIN

COOKING TIME: 20 MIN

SERVINGS: 4

WHOLE RYE TOAST WITH AVOCADO AND TOMATO

Ingredients

- 4 slices of rye bread
- 1 ripe avocado
- 1 large ripe tomato
- Salt and pepper, to taste
- Optional: a drizzle of olive oil or a squeeze of lemon juice

Directions

1. Toast the rye bread until it's golden and crispy. While toasting, slice the avocado and tomato. Once the toast is ready, top each slice with avocado and tomato.
2. Powder with salt and crushed pepper and, if you like, a drizzle of olive oil or a squeeze of lemon juice.
3. Again, the nutritional information can vary based on your ingredients.

Nutritions

250 calories, 15g Fat, 7g Protein, 25g Carbohydrate per serving

PREPARATION TIME: 10 MIN

COOKING TIME: 2 MIN

SERVINGS: 2

WARM BARLEY AND BERRY BREAKFAST

Ingredients

- 1 cup barley
- 3 cups water
- 2 cups mixed berries
- Honey or maple syrup, to taste

Directions

1. Rinse the barley under water until it runs clear. In a saucepan, add water to a boil. Add the barley and reduce the heat to low, cover, and simmer for 41-45 minutes or until the barley is tender.
2. Divide the cooked barley into four bowls, top each with a half cup of mixed berries, and sweeten with honey or maple syrup to taste.

Nutritions

230 calories, 3g Fat, 6g Protein, 48g Carbohydrate per serving

PREPARATION TIME: 5 MIN

COOKING TIME: 45 MIN

SERVINGS: 4

CHIA AND QUINOA PUDDING WITH FRESH FRUITS

Ingredients

- 1/4 cup chia seeds
- 1 cup almond milk
- 1/2 cup cooked quinoa
- 1 tablespoon honey or maple syrup
- 1 cup fresh fruits

Directions

1. Combine the chia seeds and almond milk in a bowl. Stir well and refrigerate overnight. In the morning, whisk the mixture and add the cooked quinoa and sweetener.
2. Divide the pudding evenly into two serving bowls and top with fresh fruits.

Nutritions

350 calories, 15g Fat, 10g Protein, 45g Carbohydrate per serving

PREPARATION TIME: 10 MIN

COOKING TIME: 0 MIN

SERVINGS: 2

WHOLE GRAIN BLUEBERRY MUFFINS

Ingredients

- 2 cups whole-grain flour
- 1 cup fresh blueberries
- 2 eggs
- 1/2 cup honey or maple syrup
- 1/2 cup unsweetened almond milk
- 1/4 cup melted coconut oil or olive oil
- 2 teaspoons baking powder
- Pinch of salt

Directions

1. Set the oven heat to 375°F (190°C) and arrange the muffin tin/box with paper liners. Whisk the flour with baking powder and salt in a bowl.
2. Whisk together the eggs, sweetener, milk, and oil in another bowl. Stir the wet elements into the dry, then fold the blueberries.
3. Fill the batter into the muffin cups (fill evenly) and bake for 19-20 minutes. Serve and enjoy.

Nutritions

185 calories, 6g Fat, 4g Protein, 30g Carbohydrate per muffin

PREPARATION TIME: 15 MIN

COOKING TIME: 20 MIN

SERVINGS: 12 MUFFINS

WHEAT BERRY AND VEGGIE BREAKFAST STIR-FRY

Ingredients

- 1 cup wheat berries
- 3 cups water
- 2 tablespoons olive oil
- 2 cups mixed vegetables (bell peppers, onions, tomatoes, zucchini)
- 2 cloves garlic, minced
- Salt and pepper, to taste

Directions

1. Soak the wheat berries in water overnight. Drain the wheat berries and rinse them under cold water. In a saucepan, bring the 3 cups of water to a boil. Add the wheat berries, reduce the heat to low, cover, and simmer for 41-45 minutes or until tender. Drain any remaining water.
2. Heat two tbsp oil over medium heat in a large frying pan or wok. Add the garlic and sauté until fragrant. Add the mixed vegetables and cook until they are tender.
3. Stir in the cooked wheat berries and season with salt and pepper. Cook for another 3-5 minutes until heated through.

Nutritions

310 calories, 10g Fat, 12g Protein, 47g Carbohydrate per serving

PREPARATION TIME: 10 MIN

COOKING TIME: 50 MIN

SERVINGS: 4

QUINOA AND VEGETABLE BREAKFAST HASH

Ingredients

- 1 cup cooked quinoa
- 1 tablespoon olive oil
- 1 small onion, diced
- 1 bell pepper, diced
- 1 zucchini, diced
- 2 cloves garlic, minced
- 1 teaspoon smoked paprika
- Salt and pepper, to taste

Directions

1. Over medium heat, warm one tbsp olive oil in a large skillet. Add bell pepper, zucchini, and onion. Cook the vegetables for 5-7 minutes or until they are soft. Cook for another minute after adding the smoked paprika and garlic.
2. When the quinoa is heated through, add it to the skillet and simmer for an additional 5 minutes, turning occasionally.
3. Season with salt and pepper to taste.

Nutritions

280 calories, 12g Fat, 10g Protein, 34g Carbohydrate per serving

PREPARATION TIME: 10 MIN

COOKING TIME: 20 MIN

SERVINGS: 4

MILLET PORRIDGE WITH CINNAMON APPLES

Ingredients

- 1 cup millet
- 4 cups almond milk (or milk of your choice)
- 2 apples, peeled and diced
- 1 tablespoon honey or maple syrup
- 1 teaspoon cinnamon
- Pinch of salt

Directions

1. Rinse the millet under cold water until the water runs clear. Combine the millet, almond milk, and a pinch of salt in a saucepan. Bring to a boil. Decrease the stove heat to low, cover, and simmer for 17-20 minutes.
2. While the millet is cooking, heat another saucepan over medium heat. Add the diced apples, honey or maple syrup, and cinnamon. Cook for ten minutes or until the apples are soft.
3. If desired, serve the millet porridge in bowls, topped with cinnamon apples and a drizzle of honey or maple syrup.

Nutritions

210 calories, 3g Fat, 6g Protein, 42g Carbohydrate per serving

PREPARATION TIME: 5 MIN

COOKING TIME: 20 MIN

SERVINGS: 4

BUCKWHEAT CREPES WITH SPINACH AND FETA

Ingredients

- 1 cup buckwheat flour
- 2 eggs
- 1½ cups milk (or plant-based milk)
- 1 cup fresh spinach, chopped
- 1/2 cup crumbled feta cheese
- Salt and pepper, to taste
- Olive oil for cooking

Directions

1. Whisk together the buckwheat flour, eggs, milk, salt, and pepper in a large mixing bowl until smooth. Stir in the chopped spinach and crumbled feta cheese.
2. Put the crepe pan over medium heat and lightly brush it with olive oil. Pour ¼ cup of the batter onto the pan and swirl it around to form a thin crepe.
3. Cook for three minutes for each side or until lightly golden. Repeat with the remaining batter.
4. Serve the buckwheat crepes with your fillings, such as sautéed vegetables, additional cheese, or Greek yogurt.

Nutritions

Calories: 280, Fat: 12g, Protein: 10g, Carbohydrate: 34g per serving

PREPARATION TIME: 10 MIN

COOKING TIME: 20 MIN

SERVINGS: 4

WHOLE GRAIN TACOS WITH AVOCADO AND BEANS

Ingredients

- 4 small whole-grain tortillas
- 1 avocado, sliced
- 1 cup cooked black beans
- 1 cup diced tomatoes
- ¼ cup chopped fresh cilantro
- ½ lime, juiced
- Salt and pepper, to taste

Directions

1. Warm the tortillas as directed by package instructions. Combine the sliced avocado, black beans, diced tomatoes, cilantro, lime juice, salt, and crushed pepper in a bowl.
2. Divide the avocado and bean mixture evenly among the tortillas. Serve the breakfast tacos immediately and enjoy!

Nutritions

Calories: 320, Fat: 15g, Protein: 12g, Carbohydrate: 38g per serving

PREPARATION TIME: 10 MIN

COOKING TIME: 10 MIN

SERVINGS: 2

BULGUR WHEAT PORRIDGE WITH RAISINS AND ALMONDS

Ingredients

- 1/2 cup bulgur wheat
- 1 cup water
- 1 cup milk (or plant-based milk)
- 2 tablespoons raisins
- 2 tablespoons sliced almonds
- 1 tablespoon honey or maple syrup
- Cinnamon, to taste

Directions

1. In a saucepan, add water to a boil. Add the bulgur wheat and reduce the heat to low. Cover and simmer for 10-12 minutes until the bulgur is tender.
2. Stir in the milk, raisins, sliced almonds, honey, or maple syrup, and cinnamon. Cook for 2-3 minutes, stirring occasionally, until heated through.
3. Serve the bulgur wheat porridge warm and enjoy.

Nutritions

Calories: 280, Fat: 7g, Protein: 8g, Carbohydrate: 50g per serving

PREPARATION TIME: 5 MIN

COOKING TIME: 15 MIN

SERVINGS: 2

TOAST WITH NUT BUTTER AND BANANA

Ingredients

- 4 slices of whole grain bread, toasted
- 4 tablespoons nut butter (such as almond butter or peanut butter)
- 1 banana, sliced
- Optional toppings: chia seeds, hemp seeds, or a drizzle of honey

Directions

1. Toast the slices of whole grain bread. Spread 1 tablespoon of nut butter onto each slice of toast. Top each with a sliced banana and any of the optional toppings of your choice.
2. Serve the whole grain toast with nut butter and banana immediately.

Nutritions

Calories: 260, Fat: 11g, Protein: 8g, Carbohydrate: 35g per serving

PREPARATION TIME: 5 MIN

COOKING TIME: 0 MIN

SERVINGS: 2

MILLET AND BERRY SMOOTHIE BOWL

Ingredients

- 1 cup cooked millet, cooled
- 1 frozen banana
- 1 cup mixed berries
- ½ cup almond milk (or milk of your choice)
- Toppings: fresh berries, sliced almonds, chia seeds, or shredded coc

Directions

1. Combine the cooked millet, frozen banana, mixed berries, and almond milk in a blender. Blend until smooth and creamy.
2. Pour the smoothie into the serving bowl and top with your desired toppings. Enjoy the millet and berry smoothie bowl immediately.

Nutritions

Calories: 320, Fat: 6g, Protein: 8g, Carbohydrate: 63g per serving

PREPARATION TIME: 5 MIN

COOKING TIME: 0 MIN

SERVINGS: 2

APPLE CINNAMON WHOLE GRAIN PANCAKES

Ingredients

- 1 cup whole-grain flour
- 1 teaspoon baking powder
- 1/2 teaspoon ground cinnamon
- 1 cup almond milk
- 1 tablespoon honey or maple syrup
- 1 apple, grated
- 1 egg
- 1 tablespoon coconut oil or butter for cooking

Directions

1. Whisk the whole-grain flour with baking powder, and ground cinnamon in a large mixing bowl. Whisk together the almond milk, honey or maple syrup, grated apple, and egg in a separate bowl.
2. Pour the wet elements into the dry and stir until just combined. Refrain from overmixing; the batter may be slightly lumpy. Pour the non-stick frying pan or griddle over medium heat and melt the coconut oil or butter.
3. Pour about ¼ cup of batter onto the pan for each pancake. Cook for 2-3 minutes for each side until golden brown is cooked. Serve the apple cinnamon whole grain pancakes warm and enjoy.

Nutritions

Calories: 260, Fat: 6g, Protein: 8g, Carbohydrate: 46g per serving

PREPARATION TIME: 10 MIN

COOKING TIME: 15 MIN

SERVINGS: 4

MEDITERRANEAN BURRITOS WITH TOMATO AND CHEESE

Ingredients

- 2 whole grain tortillas
- 4 eggs
- 1/2 cup diced tomatoes
- 1/4 cup chopped fresh herbs (such as parsley or basil)
- 1/4 cup crumbled feta cheese
- Salt and pepper, to taste
- Olive oil for cooking

Directions

1. Whisk the eggs with the diced tomatoes, chopped fresh herbs, crumbled feta cheese, salt, and pepper in a bowl. Put the non-stick frying pan over moderate heat and drizzle with olive oil.
2. Add egg mixture into the frypan and scramble until cooked through. Warm the whole-grain tortillas in a separate pan or microwave.
3. Divide the scrambled egg mixture between the tortillas and fold them into burritos. Serve the Mediterranean breakfast burritos immediately and enjoy.

Nutritions

Calories: 320, Fat: 12g, Protein: 12g, Carbohydrate: 45g per serving

PREPARATION TIME: 10 MIN

COOKING TIME: 10 MIN

SERVINGS: 2

SAVORY OATMEAL WITH SAUTEED VEGETABLES

Ingredients

- 1 cup rolled oats
- 2 cups water or vegetable broth
- 1 tablespoon olive oil
- 1 small onion, diced
- 1 bell pepper, diced
- 1 zucchini, diced
- 2 cloves garlic, minced
- Salt and pepper, to taste
- Optional toppings: sliced avocado, chopped fresh herbs

Directions

1. In a saucepan, bring the water or vegetable broth to a boil. Add the rolled oats and cook according to the package instructions. While the oats are cooking, heat the olive oil in the other pan over medium heat.
2. Sauté the diced onion, bell pepper, zucchini, and minced garlic until tender. Season the sautéed vegetables with salt and pepper. Serve the cooked oats in bowls, topped with the sautéed vegetables.
3. Garnish with sliced avocado and chopped fresh herbs, if desired. Enjoy the savory oatmeal while warm.

Nutritions

Calories: 280, Fat: 8g, Protein: 9g, Carbohydrate: 45g per serving

PREPARATION TIME: 10 MIN

COOKING TIME: 15 MIN

SERVINGS: 2

OVERNIGHT CHIA PUDDING WITH QUINOA AND BERRIES

Ingredients

- 1/4 cup chia seeds
- 1 cup almond milk
- 1/2 cup cooked quinoa, cooled
- 1 cup mixed berries
- 1 tablespoon honey or maple syrup
- Optional toppings: sliced almonds, shredded coconut, or additional b

Directions

1. In a bowl or jar, combine the chia seeds and almond milk. Stir well. Add the cooked quinoa and mix until well combined. Cover the bowl/jar and refrigerate overnight or 4 hours at least.
2. In the morning, stir the chia pudding. If desired, add more almond milk to achieve your desired consistency. Layer the chia pudding with mixed berries in serving glasses or bowls.
3. Drizzle honey or maple syrup and sprinkle with optional toppings, if desired.
4. Enjoy the overnight chia pudding with quinoa and chilled berries.

Nutritions

Calories: 320, Fat: 9g, Protein: 9g, Carbohydrate: 51g per serving

PREPARATION TIME: 5 MIN

COOKING TIME: 0 MIN

SERVINGS: 2

RYE BREAD WITH SMASHED AVOCADO AND POACHED EGG

Ingredients

- 4 slices of whole rye bread, toasted
- 1 ripe avocado
- 2 poached eggs
- Salt and pepper, to taste
- Optional toppings: red pepper flakes, fresh herbs, or a squeeze of lem

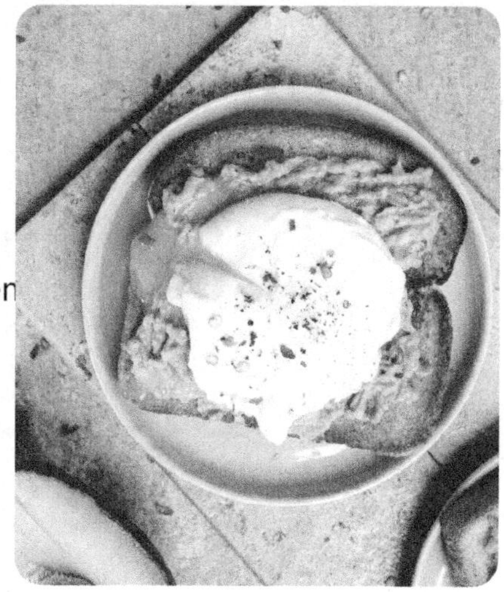

Directions

1. Toast the slices of whole rye bread until golden and crispy. Cut the ripe avocado in half to remove the pit. Scoop out the flesh into a bowl. Smash the avocado, then season with salt and pepper.
2. Spread the smashed seasoned avocado onto each slice of toasted rye bread. Top each slice with a poached egg. Garnish with optional toppings, such as red pepper flakes, fresh herbs, or a squeeze of lemon juice.
3. Serve the toasted whole rye bread with smashed avocado and poached egg immediately.

Nutritions

Calories: 300, Fat: 15g, Protein: 12g, Carbohydrate: 30g per serving

PREPARATION TIME: 10 MIN

COOKING TIME: 5 MIN

SERVINGS: 2

Chapter 4:

20 Mediterranean-Style Meat Recipes

MEDITERRANEAN BEEF AND VEGETABLE STIR-FRY

Ingredients

- 1 lb lean beef, thinly sliced
- 1 tablespoon olive oil
- 1 red bell pepper, thinly sliced
- 1 yellow bell pepper, thinly sliced
- 1 zucchini, thinly sliced
- 1 cup cherry tomatoes, halved
- 2 cloves garlic, minced
- 1 teaspoon dried oregano
- Salt and black pepper to taste
- Fresh parsley for garnish

Directions

1. Warm olive oil in a large non-stick skillet on medium-high.
2. Add and brown the beef slices for 3–4 mins. Take away the beef from the skillet and set it away.
3. Add bell peppers, zucchini, cherry tomatoes, garlic, dried oregano, salt & black pepper to the skillet. Stir-fry for 5 minutes until vegetables are tender-crisp.
4. Bring the beef cooked to the skillet for 2 minutes to heat through.
5. Garnish with fresh parsley before serving.

Nutritions

Calories: 250, Fat: 10g , Protein: 30g , Carbohydrate: 10g

PREPARATION TIME: 15 MIN

COOKING TIME: 15 MIN

SERVINGS: 4

BEEF TAGINE WITH OLIVES AND PRESERVED LEMON

Ingredients

- 2 lbs beef stew meat, chunks
- 1 onion, finely chopped
- 4 cloves garlic, minced
- 1 tablespoon olive oil
- 1 teaspoon ground cumin
- 1 teaspoon ground coriander
- 1 teaspoon ground ginger
- 1 teaspoon paprika
- 1/2 teaspoon ground cinnamon
- 1/2 teaspoon turmeric
- 1 preserved lemon, pulp removed, and rind chopped
- 1 cup pitted green olives
- 2 cups beef broth
- Salt and black pepper to taste
- Fresh cilantro for garnish

Directions

1. In a big saucepan or tagine, bring the olive oil to a temperature of medium heat.
2. Sauté the garlic and onion for a few minutes until they have become more tender.
3. After adding the beef chunks, cook them until they are browned on all sides.
4. Mix in cumin, coriander, ginger, paprika, cinnamon, turmeric, preserved lemon rind, and olives.
5. Pour the beef stock, then sprinkle with the kosher salt and ground black pepper.
6. Take the mixture to a boil, lower the heat, cover & simmer for 2 hours until the meat is cooked.
7. Before serving, garnish with freshly chopped cilantro.

Nutritions

Calories: 380, Fat: 20g , Protein: 35g , Carbohydrate: 10g

PREPARATION TIME: 20 MIN

COOKING TIME: 2 HOUR

SERVINGS: 6

MEDITERRANEAN BEEF STUFFED BELL PEPPERS

Ingredients

- 4 bell peppers, tops removed, and seeds also removed
- 1 lb lean ground beef
- 1 onion, finely chopped
- 2 cloves garlic, minced
- 1 cup cooked brown rice
- 1 cup marinara sauce
- 1 teaspoon dried oregano
- Salt and black pepper to taste
- Grated Parmesan cheese for topping
- Fresh parsley for garnish

Directions

1. Lightly grease a baking dish and preheat the oven to 375F (190
2. C).
3. Brown ground beef in a non-stick skillet over moderate heat. Remove any unnecessary fat.
4. Sauté the onion and garlic until softened in the skillet.
5. Add brown rice, marinara sauce, dried oregano, salt, and black pepper. Add two to three more minutes of cooking time.
6. Place the peppers stuffed with cheese in the prepared baking dish. The meat and rice combination can be made in advance.
7. The filled bell peppers would benefit from a sprinkle of grated Parmesan cheese.
8. Bake the foil-covered dish for 30 minutes. Remove the foil and prepare for 10-15 mins until the peppers are prepared, and the cheese is bubbling.
9. Garnish with fresh parsley before serving.

Nutritions

Calories: 320 , Fat: 10g , Protein: 25g , Carbohydrate: 30g

PREPARATION TIME: 15 MIN

COOKING TIME: 45 MIN

SERVINGS: 4

ROASTED PORK TENDERLOIN WITH OLIVES AND CAPERS

Ingredients

- 1 lb pork tenderloin
- 2 tablespoons olive oil
- 2 cloves garlic, minced
- 1 tablespoon fresh rosemary, chopped
- 1 tablespoon fresh thyme, chopped
- Salt and black pepper to taste
- 1/4 cup pitted Kalamata olives, sliced
- 1 tablespoon capers

Directions

1. To prepare a baking sheet with foil, preheat the oven to 425°F (220 degrees C).
2. Mix the minced garlic, rosemary, thyme, salt, and black pepper in a small bowl.
3. To apply the mixture to the pork tenderloin, rub it all over.
4. Roast the seasoned pork for 20–25 minutes at 145°F (63°C) on the prepared baking sheet.
5. Take the pork out of your oven and rest for a few mins before cutting it into slices.
6. Garnish the sliced pork with Kalamata olives and capers.

Nutritions

Calories: 250 , Fat: 10g , Protein: 30g , Carbohydrate: 2g

PREPARATION TIME: 10 MIN

COOKING TIME: 25 MIN

SERVINGS: 4

GRILLED PORK CHOPS WITH LEMON AND OREGANO

Ingredients

- 4 boneless pork chops
- 2 tablespoons olive oil
- 2 tablespoons fresh lemon juice
- 1 teaspoon fresh oregano, chopped
- 2 cloves garlic, minced
- Salt and black pepper to taste
- Lemon wedges for serving

Directions

1. Preheat the grill to medium-high heat.
2. Mix olive oil, lemon juice, oregano, minced garlic, salt, and black pepper in a medium-sized bowl.
3. Coat the pork pieces on both sides with the marinade.
4. Grill pork chops for 6 minutes per side until cooked through and slightly browned.
5. Before serving, remove the pork chops from the grill and allow them to settle for a few minutes.
6. Lemon wedges for squeezing over pork chops.

Nutritions

Calories: 280 , Fat: 15g , Protein: 30g , Carbohydrate: 2g

PREPARATION TIME: 10 MIN

COOKING TIME: 12 MIN

SERVINGS: 4

MEDITERRANEAN PORK AND BEAN STEW

Ingredients

- 1 lb boneless pork shoulder, cut into chunks
- 2 tablespoons olive oil
- 1 onion, chopped
- 2 cloves garlic, minced
- 1 carrot, diced
- 1 celery stalk, diced
- 1 can (14 oz) diced tomatoes
- 2 cups chicken broth
- 1 teaspoon dried oregano
- 1 teaspoon dried thyme
- 1 teaspoon paprika
- 1 can (15 oz) cannellini beans, drained and rinsed
- Salt and black pepper to taste
- Fresh parsley for garnish

Directions

1. Medium-heat olive oil in a big pot.
2. Brown pork shoulder chunks on all sides. Set meat aside.
3. Add onion, garlic, carrot, and celery to the saucepan. Sauté the veggies until they are soft.
4. Return the pork to the saucepan and add chopped tomatoes, chicken stock, dried oregano, dry thyme, and paprika. Add salt and black pepper to taste.
5. Take the mixture to a boil, lower the heat, cover, and simmer for 1 hour until the pork is cooked.
6. Add the cannellini beans to the pot and simmer for 15 minutes. Adjust the seasoning if needed.
7. Serve the stew hot, garnished with fresh parsley

Nutritions

Calories: 320 , Fat: 15g , Protein: 25g , Carbohydrate: 20g

PREPARATION TIME: 15 MIN

COOKING TIME: 1 HR 30 MIN

SERVINGS: 6

MEDITERRANEAN LAMB AND BARLEY STEW

Ingredients

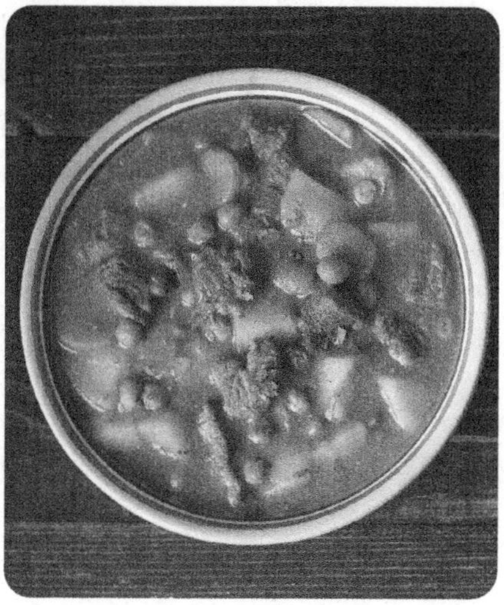

- 1 lb lamb stew meat, cut into chunks
- 2 tablespoons olive oil
- 1 onion, chopped
- 2 cloves garlic, minced
- 1 carrot, diced
- 1 celery stalk, diced
- 1 cup pearl barley
- 4 cups beef broth
- 1 teaspoon dried rosemary
- 1 teaspoon dried thyme
- Salt and black pepper to taste
- Fresh parsley for garnish

Directions

1. In a big pot, heat the olive oil over a medium-high flame. Brown lamb stew meat on all sides. Set lamb aside.
2. Add onion, garlic, carrot, and celery to the saucepan. Sauté veggies until soft.
3. Return lamb to saucepan and add pearl barley, beef broth, rosemary, thyme, salt, and black pepper.
4. Take the mixture to a boil, then decrease the heat to low, cover, and prepare for approximately an hour until the lamb and barley are soft.
5. Adjust the seasoning if needed.
6. Serve the stew hot, garnished with fresh parsley.

Nutritions

Calories: 320 , Fat: 15g , Protein: 25g , Carbohydrate: 25g

PREPARATION TIME: 15 MIN

COOKING TIME: 1 HR 30 MIN

SERVINGS: 6

MEDITERRANEAN LAMB AND VEGETABLE SKEWERS

Ingredients

- 1 lb lamb leg meat, cut into chunks
- 1 zucchini, sliced
- 1 red bell pepper, cut into chunks
- 1 red onion, cut into chunks
- 2 tablespoons olive oil
- 2 cloves garlic, minced
- 1 teaspoon dried oregano
- Juice of 1 lemon
- Salt and black pepper to taste
- Skewers for grilling

Directions

1. Combine the olive oil, minced garlic, dried oregano, lemon juice, salt, and black pepper in a bowl.
2. Add the lamb chunks to the marinade and toss to coat. Let it marinate for at least 30 mins.
3. Preheat the grill to medium-high heat.
4. Thread the marinated lamb chunks, zucchini slices, red bell pepper chunks, and red onion chunks onto skewers.
5. Grill the skewers for 10-15 mins, turning occasionally, until the lamb is prepared to your desired doneness and the vegetables are tender.
6. Remove from the grill and let the skewers rest for a few minutes before serving.

Nutritions

Calories: 280 , Fat: 15g , Protein: 30g , Carbohydrate: 8g

PREPARATION TIME: 20 MIN

COOKING TIME: 15 MIN

SERVINGS: 4

ROASTED LAMB WITH ROSEMARY AND GARLIC

Ingredients

- 2 lbs lamb leg roast
- 4 cloves garlic, minced
- 2 tablespoons fresh rosemary, chopped
- 2 tablespoons olive oil
- Salt and black pepper to taste

Directions

1. Turn the oven's temperature on and set it to 350°F (175°C).
2. Mix minced garlic, rosemary, olive oil, salt, and black pepper in a small bowl.
3. Put the rack with the lamb leg roast in a cooking pan.
4. Ensure all lamb is covered with a blend of garlic and rosemary. Roast the lamb for 1 hour 30 minutes or until done.
5. Remove the chicken from your oven and allow it to sit for 10 mins before cutting into it.
6. Serve the roasted lamb slices with your choice of side dishes.

Nutritions

Calories: 360 , Fat: 18g , Protein: 45g , Carbohydrate: 0g

PREPARATION TIME: 10 MIN

COOKING TIME: 1 HR 30 MIN

SERVINGS: 4

GREEK LEMON CHICKEN SOUP (AVGOLEMONO)

Ingredients

- 4 cups chicken broth
- 2 cups cooked chicken breast, shredded
- 1/2 cup orzo pasta
- 3 eggs
- Juice of 2 lemons
- Salt and black pepper to taste
- Fresh dill for garnish

Directions

1. Bring the chicken bouillon to a boil in a pot. Cook orzo pasta al dente according to package directions.
2. Stir in the chicken breast and heat for a few minutes in a simmering sauce.
3. Whisk together the eggs & lemon juice in a separate basin until thoroughly combined.
4. Slowly add a ladleful of boiling broth while continuously whisking the egg-lemon mixture.
5. Pour the egg-lemon mixture back into the pot slowly, stirring. Simmer for 2-3 minutes to thicken the soup.
6. Use salt and black pepper for seasoning to taste. Serve the soup hot, garnished with fresh dill.

Nutritions

Calories: 250 , Fat: 7g , Protein: 25g , Carbohydrate: 20g

PREPARATION TIME: 10 MIN

COOKING TIME: 30 MIN

SERVINGS: 4

CHICKEN SOUVLAKI WITH GREEK SALAD

Ingredients

- 1 lb chicken breast, cut into cubes
- 2 tablespoons olive oil
- Juice of 1 lemon
- 2 cloves garlic, minced
- 1 teaspoon dried oregano
- Salt and black pepper to taste
- 4 pita bread rounds
- Greek Salad:
- 2 cups cherry tomatoes, halved
- 1 cucumber, diced
- 1/2 red onion, thinly sliced
- 1/2 cup Kalamata olives
- 1/2 cup feta cheese, crumbled
- 2 tablespoons olive oil
- Juice of 1 lemon
- Salt and black pepper to taste
- Fresh parsley for garnish

Directions

1. Mix olive oil, lemon juice, minced garlic, dried oregano, salt & black pepper in a bowl.
2. Toss marinade-coated chicken cubes. 30-minute marinate.
3. Set the grill or grill pan to a medium-high setting to get it ready.
4. Grill cubes of marinated chicken for 8 to 10 minutes, turning periodically, until cooked and lightly charred.
5. Prepare the Greek salad while cooking the chicken. Mix feta, cherry tomatoes, cucumbers, red onions, and Kalamata olives in a large bowl.
6. Drizzle olive oil and lemon juice, then season with salt and black pepper. Toss to combine.
7. Warm the pita bread rounds on the grill for a few seconds on each side.
8. Serve the grilled chicken souvlaki with the Greek salad and warm pita bread.
9. Garnish with fresh parsley.

Nutritions

Calories: 380 , Fat: 15g , Protein: 35g , Carbohydrate: 25g

PREPARATION TIME: 20 MIN

COOKING TIME: 10 MIN

SERVINGS: 4

MEDITERRANEAN CHICKEN AND VEGETABLE STIR-FRY

Ingredients

- 1 lb chicken breast, sliced
- 2 tablespoons olive oil
- 2 cloves garlic, minced
- 1 onion, sliced
- 1 red bell pepper, sliced
- 1 zucchini, sliced
- 1 cup cherry tomatoes, halved
- 1 tablespoon lemon juice
- 1 teaspoon dried oregano
- Salt and black pepper to taste
- Fresh parsley for garnish

Directions

1. Warm olive oil in a large non-stick skillet or wok over medium-high heat.
2. Add the minced garlic and sliced onion to the skillet and sauté for 2-3 mins until the onion is translucent.
3. Add the sliced chicken breast to the skillet and cook for about 5-6 minutes until it is cooked.
4. Add the sliced red bell pepper and zucchini to the skillet and stir-fry for 2-3 mins until the vegetables are crisp-tender.
5. Stir in the cherry tomatoes, lemon juice, dried oregano, salt, and black pepper. Cook for another minute to heat through.
6. Take it off the heat and sprinkle fresh parsley on top.
7. Serve the Mediterranean chicken and vegetable stir-fry hot.

Nutritions

Calories: 280 , Fat: 10g , Protein: 35g , Carbohydrate: 10g

PREPARATION TIME:15 MIN

COOKING TIME: 15 MIN

SERVINGS: 4

CHICKEN TAGINE WITH OLIVES AND PRESERVED LEMON

Ingredients

- 1 whole chicken, cut into pieces
- 2 tablespoons olive oil
- 1 onion, chopped
- 3 cloves garlic, minced
- 1 teaspoon ground cumin
- 1 teaspoon ground coriander
- 1/2 teaspoon ground ginger
- 1/2 teaspoon ground cinnamon
- 1/2 teaspoon turmeric
- 1 preserved lemon, pulp removed, rind rinsed and chopped
- 1 cup green olives
- 1 cup chicken broth
- Salt and black pepper to taste
- Fresh cilantro for garnish

Directions

1. Medium-heat olive oil in a big pot or tagine. In a saucepan, sauté the chopped onion and minced garlic until transparent, about 2 to 3 minutes.
2. Add the chicken pieces to the pot and brown them on both sides.
3. Combine ground cumin, coriander, ginger, cinnamon, and turmeric. Toast spices for another minute.
4. Preserved lemon, green olives, and chicken broth in the pot. Salt and black pepper to taste.
5. Boil the mixture, lower the heat, and cover the pot.
6. Simmer the chicken for 1 hour and 30 minutes.
7. Garnish with fresh cilantro before serving.
8. Serve the chicken tagine hot with your choice of side dishes.

Nutritions

Calories: 350 , Fat: 18g , Protein: 30g , Carbohydrate: 12g

PREPARATION TIME: 15 MIN

COOKING TIME: 1 HR 30 MIN

SERVINGS: 4

MEDITERRANEAN CHICKEN AND ORZO SALAD

Ingredients

- 2 cups cooked chicken breast, shredded
- 1 cup cooked orzo pasta
- 1 cucumber, diced
- 1 red bell pepper, diced
- 1/2 red onion, thinly sliced
- 1/2 cup Kalamata olives, pitted & halved
- 1/4 cup crumbled feta cheese
- 2 tablespoons olive oil
- Juice of 1 lemon
- 1 teaspoon dried oregano
- Salt and black pepper to taste
- Fresh parsley for garnish

Directions

1. Combine the chicken breast, cooked orzo pasta, diced cucumber, red bell pepper, sliced red onion, Kalamata olives, and crumbled feta cheese in a bowl.
2. Whisk together the olive oil, lemon juice, dried oregano, salt & black pepper in a separate small bowl.
3. Pour the sauce over the salad, then toss it to mix everything.
4. Garnish with fresh parsley before serving.
5. Serve the Mediterranean chicken and orzo salad chilled or at room temperature.

Nutritions

Calories: 320 , Fat: 12g , Protein: 25g , Carbohydrate: 25g

PREPARATION TIME: 20 MIN

COOKING TIME: 15 MIN

SERVINGS: 4

CHICKEN PAELLA WITH SAFFRON AND OLIVES

Ingredients

- 1 lb chicken thighs, bone-in, and skin-on
- 2 tablespoons olive oil
- 1 onion, chopped
- 3 cloves garlic, minced
- 1 red bell pepper, sliced
- 1 yellow bell pepper, sliced
- 1 cup Arborio rice
- 1/2 teaspoon saffron threads
- 1 teaspoon smoked paprika
- 1/2 teaspoon dried thyme
- 1/2 teaspoon dried oregano
- 1/2 cup white wine
- 2 cups chicken broth
- 1/2 cup green peas
- 1/2 cup pitted green olives
- Salt and black pepper to taste
- Lemon wedges for serving
- Fresh parsley for garnish

Directions

1. Warm olive oil in a non-stick large skillet or paella pan over medium-high heat.
2. Salt and black pepper the chicken legs, then put the skin-side down in the pan. The skin should get golden brown and crispy after 5 minutes. Flip and cook for 3 minutes. Set aside.
3. Add chopped onion, minced garlic, and sliced red and yellow bell peppers to the pan. Sauté until softened.
4. Add the Arborio rice, saffron, smoked paprika, dried thyme, and oregano. Toast the spices for one more minute and stir them into the rice.
5. Pour in the white wine & allow it to cook until most of it is gone.
6. Put the chicken stock in the pan and turn the heat low. Place the chicken thighs in the rice mixture. Simmer the rice and chicken for 20–25 minutes covered.
7. Add green peas and pitted olives. Cook for additional 5 mins or until the food is fully warm. Let it cool for a few minutes.
8. Serve the chicken paella hot, garnished with fresh parsley and lemon wedges.

Nutritions

Calories: 420 , Fat: 15g , Protein: 30g , Carbohydrate: 40g

PREPARATION TIME: 15 MIN

COOKING TIME: 40 MIN

SERVINGS: 4

BAKED CHICKEN WITH ARTICHOKES AND CAPERS

Ingredients

- 4 chicken breasts
- 1 tablespoon olive oil
- 2 cloves garlic, minced
- 1 can artichoke hearts, drained and quartered
- 2 tablespoons capers
- Juice of 1 lemon
- 1 teaspoon dried oregano
- Salt and black pepper to taste
- Fresh parsley for garnish

Directions

1. Set the oven's temperature to 400°F (200°C).
2. Add salt and black pepper to the chicken breasts, and set them aside.
3. Medium-high heat olive oil in an oven-safe pan. Brown the chicken breasts in the skillet for 3–4 minutes per side.
4. Please take out the chicken from the pan and put it to the side for later.
5. Sauté minced garlic in the same skillet for 1 minute until fragrant.
6. Artichoke hearts, capers, lemon juice, dried oregano, salt, and black pepper to the skillet. Stir to combine.
7. Place the chicken breasts in the pan on the artichoke mixture. Prepare for 20–25 mins in the preheated oven.
8. Garnish with fresh parsley before serving.
9. Serve the baked chicken with artichokes and capers hot.

Nutritions

Calories: 280 , Fat: 8g , Protein: 40g , Carbohydrate: 8g

PREPARATION TIME: 10 MIN

COOKING TIME: 30 MIN

4SERVINGS: 2

TURKEY AND VEGETABLE STUFFED PEPPERS

Ingredients

- 4 bell peppers (any color)
- 1 lb ground turkey
- 1 small onion, finely chopped
- 2 cloves garlic, minced
- 1 zucchini, diced
- 1 yellow squash, diced
- 1 cup cooked quinoa
- 1 teaspoon dried oregano
- 1 teaspoon dried basil
- Salt and black pepper to taste
- 1 cup marinara sauce
- Fresh parsley for garnish

Directions

1. Turn the oven on and place it to 375°F (190°C).
2. Remove bell pepper seeds and membranes. Put them away.
3. Brown the ground turkey in a big pan that doesn't stick over medium heat. Get rid of any extra fat.
4. Sauté chopped onion and minced garlic in the skillet for 2-3 minutes until aromatic.
5. Cook the diced zucchini and yellow squash for 5 more minutes.
6. Add cooked quinoa, dried oregano, basil, salt, and black pepper. Mix well.
7. Put the turkey and vegetables in the bell peppers.
8. Marinara sauce over stuffed peppers in a baking dish.
9. Cover the dish with foil and prepare it for 30–35 mins, or until the peppers are soft.
10. Garnish with fresh parsley before serving.
11. Serve the turkey and vegetable stuffed peppers hot.

Nutritions

Calories: 280 , Fat: 7g , Protein: 30g , Carbohydrate: 26g

PREPARATION TIME: 15 MIN

COOKING TIME: 40 MIN

SERVINGS: 4

MEDITERRANEAN TURKEY AND QUINOA STUFFED EGGPLANT

Ingredients

- 2 large eggplants
- 1 lb ground turkey
- 1 small onion, finely chopped
- 2 cloves garlic, minced
- 1 red bell pepper, diced
- 1 zucchini, diced
- 1 cup cooked quinoa
- 1 teaspoon dried oregano
- 1 teaspoon dried basil
- Salt and black pepper to taste
- 1 cup marinara sauce
- Fresh parsley for garnish

Directions

1. Turn the oven's heat on and set it to 375°F (190°C).
2. Half the eggplants are along their length. Remove the flesh, leaving a 1/2-inch shell. Set the shells of the eggplants away.
3. Cut the meat of the aubergine that you took out into small pieces.
4. Brown ground turkey in a skillet over medium heat. Get rid of any extra fat.
5. Sauté chopped onion and minced garlic in the skillet for 2-3 minutes until aromatic.
6. Combine the diced red pepper, zucchini, and eggplant in a skillet. Cook for another 5 minutes until softened.
7. Stir in the cooked quinoa, dried oregano, dried basil, salt, and black pepper. Mix well to combine.
8. Stuff the eggplant shells with the turkey and vegetable mixture.
9. Pour the marinara sauce over the stuffed eggplants in a baking dish.
10. Cover the dish with foil and prepare for 30-35 minutes until the eggplants are tender.
11. Garnish with fresh parsley before serving.
12. Serve the Mediterranean turkey and quinoa stuffed eggplant hot.

Nutritions

Calories: 320 , Fat: 9g , Protein: 28g , Carbohydrate: 32g

PREPARATION TIME: 20 MIN

COOKING TIME: 40 MIN

SERVINGS: 24

TURKEY MEATBALLS WITH TOMATO AND BASIL SAUCE

Ingredients

- 1 lb ground turkey
- 1/2 cup whole wheat breadcrumbs
- 1/4 cup grated Parmesan cheese
- 1/4 cup chopped fresh parsley
- 2 cloves garlic, minced
- 1 egg, beaten
- Salt and black pepper to taste
- 1 tablespoon olive oil
- 1 can (14 oz) crushed tomatoes
- 1 teaspoon dried basil
- 1/2 teaspoon dried oregano
- Fresh basil leaves for garnish

Directions

1. Combine the ground turkey, breadcrumbs, grated Parmesan cheese, chopped parsley, minced garlic, beaten egg, salt, and black pepper in a large bowl. Mix well to combine.
2. Make meatballs about 1 inch in diameter from the mixture.
3. Medium-heat olive oil in a skillet. Add the meatballs and cook them until all sides are cooked.
4. Mix crushed tomatoes, dried basil, dried oregano, salt, and black pepper in another pot. Simmer for 10 minutes to blend flavors. Simmer the tomato sauce and meatballs for 10 minutes.
5. Garnish with fresh basil leaves before serving. Serve the turkey meatballs with tomato and hot basil sauce.

Nutritions

Calories: 240 , Fat: 9g , Protein: 28g , Carbohydrate: 12g

PREPARATION TIME: 15 MIN

COOKING TIME: 25 MIN

SERVINGS: 4

GRILLED TURKEY SKEWERS WITH GARLIC AND HERBS

Ingredients

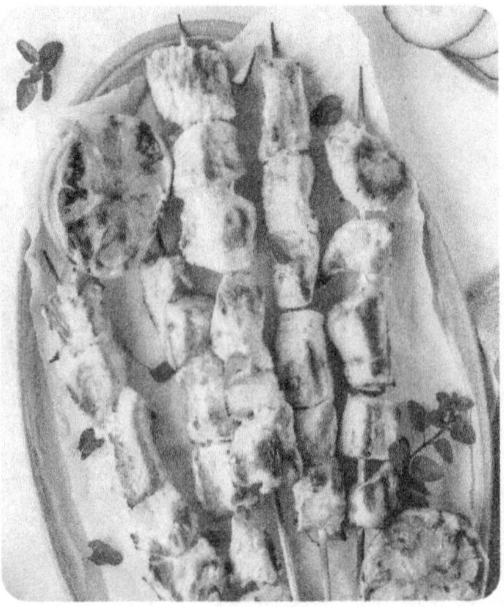

- 1 lb turkey, breast, cut into cubes
- 2 cloves garlic, minced
- 2 tablespoons chopped fresh parsley
- 2 tablespoons chopped fresh rosemary
- 2 tablespoons lemon juice
- 1 tablespoon olive oil
- Salt and black pepper to taste
- Wooden skewers soaked in water

Directions

1. Combine the minced garlic, chopped parsley, rosemary, lemon juice, olive oil, salt & black pepper in a bowl. Mix well to create a marinade.
2. Add the turkey cubes to the marinade and toss to coat evenly. Allow it to marinate for 30 mins or refrigerate overnight for enhanced flavor.
3. Preheat the grill to medium-high heat. Thread the marinated turkey cubes onto the soaked wooden skewers.
4. Put the skewers on a hot grill and cook for about 12-15 mins, turning them occasionally until the turkey is done and has a little char.
5. Take the skewers off the fire and give them a few minutes to cool down.
6. Serve the grilled turkey skewers with garlic and herbs hot.

Nutritions

Calories: 190 , Fat: 6g , Protein: 30g , Carbohydrate: 2g

PREPARATION TIME: 15 MIN

COOKING TIME: 25 MIN

SERVINGS: 4

Chapter

5: 20 Fish and Seafood Recipes

GRILLED SALMON WITH LEMON AND DILL

Ingredients

- 4 salmon fillets
- Juice of 1 lemon
- 2 tablespoons chopped fresh dill
- 1 tablespoon olive oil
- Salt and black pepper to taste

Directions

1. Preheat the grill to medium-high heat. Whisk the lemon juice, chopped dill, olive oil, salt, and black pepper in a bowl. Brush the salmon fillets with the lemon and dill mixture, coating both sides.
2. Place the salmon fillets and cook for 6 minutes for each side until it flakes easily. Remove the salmon and rest it for a few minutes before serving.
3. Serve the grilled salmon with lemon and dill hot

Nutritions

Calories: 280 , Fat: 15g , Protein: 34g , Carbohydrate: 1g

PREPARATION TIME: 10 MIN

COOKING TIME: 12 MIN

SERVINGS: 4

GREEK-STYLE SHRIMP WITH TOMATOES AND FETA

Ingredients

- 1 lb. shrimp, peeled and deveined
- 2 tablespoons olive oil
- 4 cloves garlic, minced
- 1 onion, diced
- 1 red bell pepper, diced
- 1 can (14 oz) diced tomatoes
- 1 teaspoon dried oregano
- Salt and black pepper to taste
- ½ cup crumbled feta cheese
- Fresh parsley for garnish

Directions

1. In a non-stick skillet, heat two tbsp oil over medium heat. Add the minced garlic, diced onion, and diced red bell pepper. Sauté until the vegetables are tender. Add shrimp and cook until they are cooked thoroughly.
2. Stir in the diced tomatoes, dried oregano, salt, and black pepper. Simmer for 5 minutes to allow the flavors to meld. Sprinkle the crumbled feta cheese over the shrimp and tomato mixture.
3. Cover the skillet and cook for 2-3 minutes until the feta cheese is slightly melted. Garnish with fresh parsley before serving. Serve the Greek-style shrimp with tomatoes and hot feta.

Nutritions

Calories: 220 , Fat: 11g , Protein: 26g , Carbohydrate: 7g

PREPARATION TIME: 10 MIN

COOKING TIME: 15 MIN

SERVINGS: 4

MEDITERRANEAN BAKED COD WITH OLIVES AND CAPERS

Ingredients

- 4 cod fillets
- 2 tablespoons olive oil
- 1 tablespoon lemon juice
- 2 cloves garlic, minced
- 1/4 cup pitted Kalamata olives, chopped
- 1 tablespoon capers
- 1 teaspoon dried oregano
- Salt and black pepper to taste

Directions

1. Set the oven heat to 400°F (200°C). Put the cod fillets in a baking dish. Whisk the olive oil with lemon juice, minced garlic, chopped Kalamata olives, capers, dried oregano, salt, and black pepper in a bowl.
2. Pour the olive and caper mixture over the cod fillets, ensuring they are evenly coated. Bake for 17-20 minutes until the fish is opaque and flakes easily with a fork. Remove the baked cod and rest it for a few minutes before serving.
3. Serve the Mediterranean baked cod with olives and capers hot.

Nutritions

Calories: 170 , Fat: 7g , Protein: 23g , Carbohydrate: 2g

PREPARATION TIME: 10 MIN

COOKING TIME: 20 MIN

SERVINGS: 4

SEAFOOD PAELLA WITH SAFFRON AND BELL PEPPERS

Ingredients

- 1 lb mixed seafood (shrimp, mussels, clams)
- 2 tablespoons olive oil
- 1 onion, diced
- 1 red bell pepper, diced
- 1 yellow bell pepper, diced
- 2 cloves garlic, minced
- 1 cup Arborio rice
- 2 cups vegetable broth
- 1/2 teaspoon saffron threads
- 1 teaspoon smoked paprika
- Salt and black pepper to taste
- Fresh parsley for garnish
- Lemon wedges for serving

Directions

1. Heat two tbsp oil over medium heat in a non-stick skillet or paella pan. Add diced onion and diced red & yellow bell pepper. Sauté until the vegetables are tender. Add minced garlic & Arborio rice to the skillet. Cook for 2 minutes, stirring constantly.
2. In the other saucepan, heat the vegetable broth until simmering. Add the saffron threads and smoked paprika to the broth and let it infuse for a few minutes. Gradually add the infused vegetable broth to the skillet, about ½ cup at a time, stirring well after each addition.
3. Allow the rice to absorb the broth before adding more. After about 20 minutes, add the mixed seafood to the skillet when the rice is almost cooked. Cook for 5-7 minutes until the seafood is cooked and the rice is tender.
4. Spread with salt and crushed pepper to taste. Garnish with fresh parsley and serve the seafood paella with saffron and bell peppers hot, accompanied by lemon wedges.

Nutritions

Calories: 320 , Fat: 6g , Protein: 27g , Carbohydrate: 39g

PREPARATION TIME: 15 MIN

COOKING TIME: 35 MIN

SERVINGS: 4

TUSCAN-STYLE TUNA SALAD WITH WHITE BEANS

Ingredients

- 2 cans (5 oz each weight) of tuna, drained
- 1 can (15 oz) cannellini beans, drained and rinsed
- 1 cup cherry tomatoes, halved
- 1/2 red onion, thinly sliced
- 1/4 cup chopped fresh parsley
- 2 tablespoons lemon juice
- 2 tablespoons extra-virgin olive oil
- Salt and black pepper to taste
- Mixed salad greens for serving

Directions

1. Combine the tuna, cannellini beans, cherry tomatoes, red onion, and chopped parsley in a bowl. Whisk the lemon juice with olive oil, salt, and crushed pepper in a bowl.
2. Pour the lemon oil dressing over the tuna and bean mixture and toss gently to combine.
3. Serve the Tuscan-style tuna salad over a bed of mixed salad greens.

Nutritions

Calories: 250 , Fat: 9g , Protein: 26g , Carbohydrate: 18g

PREPARATION TIME: 10 MIN

COOKING TIME: 0 MIN

SERVINGS: 4

MEDITERRANEAN SHRIMP AND ORZO SOUP

Ingredients

- 1 tablespoon olive oil
- 1 onion, diced
- 2 carrots, diced
- 2 celery stalks, diced
- 3 cloves garlic, minced
- 1 can (14 oz) diced tomatoes
- 4 cups vegetable broth
- 1/2 cup orzo pasta
- 1 lb shrimp, peeled and deveined
- 1 teaspoon dried oregano
- Salt and black pepper to taste
- Fresh parsley for garnish

Directions

1. In a non-stick stockpot, heat one tbsp olive oil over medium heat. Add diced onion, carrots, celery, and minced garlic. Sauté until the vegetables are tender. Add diced tomatoes with vegetable broth and orzo pasta.
2. Take this mixture to a boil, then decrease the stove heat and simmer for 10 minutes. Add shrimp and cook for 5-7 minutes until cooked thoroughly. Stir in the dried oregano, salt, and black pepper.
3. Ladle the Mediterranean shrimp and orzo soup into bowls and garnish with fresh parsley before serving.

Nutritions

Calories: 290 , Fat: 5g , Protein: 28g , Carbohydrate: 32g

PREPARATION TIME: 10 MIN

COOKING TIME: 25 MIN

SERVINGS: 4

BAKED MUSSELS WITH TOMATO AND GARLIC SAUCE

Ingredients

- 2 lb. mussels, cleaned and debearded
- 2 tablespoons olive oil
- 4 cloves garlic, minced
- 1 can (14 oz) diced tomatoes
- ¼ cup chopped fresh parsley
- Salt and black pepper to taste
- Lemon wedges for serving

Directions

1. Set the oven heat to 425°F (220°C). In a non-stick skillet, heat two tbsp oil over medium heat. Add minced garlic and sauté for 1-2 minutes until fragrant. Stir in the diced tomatoes, chopped parsley, salt, and black pepper.
2. Simmer for 5 minutes to allow the flavors to meld. Arrange the cleaned mussels in a single layer in a baking dish. Pour the tomato and garlic sauce over the mussels. Cover the baking dish with aluminum foil paper and bake for 10-12 minutes.
3. Discard any unopened mussels before serving. Serve the baked mussels with tomato and garlic sauce hot, accompanied by lemon wedges.

Nutritions

Calories: 180 , Fat: 6g , Protein: 20g , Carbohydrate: 10g

PREPARATION TIME: 15 MIN

COOKING TIME: 15 MIN

SERVINGS: 4

SARDINES WITH LEMON AND OLIVE OIL

Ingredients

- 4 fresh sardine fillets
- 1 lemon, sliced
- 2 tablespoons extra-virgin olive oil
- Salt and black pepper to taste

Directions

1. Preheat the grill/broiler or grill pan to high heat. Powder the sardine fillets with salt and crushed pepper. Place the sardine fillets on a grill pan or a baking sheet lined with foil. Top each with a slice of lemon, then drizzle with olive oil.
2. Grill or broil the sardines for 3-4 minutes for each side until thoroughly cooked. Serve the sardines with lemon and olive oil hot.

Nutritions

Calories: 180 , Fat: 12g , Protein: 18g , Carbohydrate: 2g

PREPARATION TIME: 5 MIN

COOKING TIME: 5 MIN

SERVINGS: 2

SEA BASS WITH MEDITERRANEAN SALSA

Ingredients

- 2 sea bass fillets
- 1 tablespoon olive oil
- 1 teaspoon dried oregano
- Salt and black pepper to taste
- 1 cup cherry tomatoes, halved
- 1/2 cup diced cucumber
- 1/4 cup diced red onion
- 2 tablespoons chopped fresh parsley
- 1 tablespoon lemon juice
- 1 tablespoon extra-virgin olive oil

Directions

1. Set the oven heat to 400°F (200°C). Put the sea bass fillets on the roasting sheet lined with foil. Drizzle with oil and sprinkle with dried oregano, salt, and black pepper. Bake the sea bass for 12-15 minutes until cooked thoroughly.
2. Combine the cherry tomatoes, diced cucumber, red onion, chopped parsley, lemon juice, and extra-virgin olive oil in a bowl. Toss to combine. Serve the sea bass with the Mediterranean salsa on top.

Nutritions

Calories: 220 , Fat: 9g , Protein: 30g , Carbohydrate: 6g

PREPARATION TIME: 10 MIN

COOKING TIME: 15 MIN

SERVINGS: 2

SHRIMP AND FETA CHEESE ORZO

Ingredients

- 1 cup orzo pasta
- 1 lb shrimp, peeled and deveined
- 2 tablespoons olive oil
- 4 cloves garlic, minced
- 1 can (14 oz) diced tomatoes
- 1/2 cup crumbled feta cheese
- 2 tablespoons chopped fresh parsley
- Salt and black pepper to taste
- Lemon wedges for serving

Directions

1. Prepare the orzo pasta as directed by package instructions. Drain and set aside. In a non-stick skillet, heat two tbsp olive oil over medium heat. Add minced garlic and sauté for 1-2 minutes until fragrant.
2. Add shrimp and cook for 3-4 minutes until cooked thoroughly. Stir in the diced tomatoes, cooked orzo, crumbled feta cheese, chopped parsley, salt, and black pepper. Cook for 2-3 minutes to heat thoroughly. Serve the shrimp and feta cheese orzo hot, with lemon wedges on top.

Nutritions

Calories: 320 , Fat: 10g , Protein: 26g , Carbohydrate: 30g

PREPARATION TIME: 10 MIN

COOKING TIME: 20 MIN

SERVINGS: 4

MEDITERRANEAN-STYLE FISH TACOS

Ingredients

- 1 lb. white fish fillets (cod or tilapia or any other)
- 1 tablespoon olive oil
- 1 teaspoon ground cumin
- 1/2 teaspoon paprika
- 1/4 teaspoon chili powder
- Salt and black pepper to taste
- 8 small whole wheat tortillas
- Greek Yogurt Sauce:
- 1/2 cup Greek yogurt
- 2 tablespoons freshly squeezed lime juice
- 2 tablespoons chopped fresh cilantro
- Salt to taste

Directions

1. Preheat the grill over medium-high heat. Rub the fish fillets with oil, then sprinkle with cumin, paprika, chili powder, salt, and crushed pepper. Grill the fish for 3-4 minutes for each side until cooked thoroughly and flaky.
2. While the fish is grilling, warm the tortillas on the grill or in a pan. Combine Greek yogurt with lime juice, chopped cilantro, and salt in a bowl. Stir well to combine. Assemble the tacos by placing a grilled fish fillet in each tortilla and topping it with Greek yogurt sauce.
3. If desired, serve the fish tacos with additional toppings.

Nutritions

Calories: 300 , Fat: 8g , Protein: 28g , Carbohydrate: 30g

PREPARATION TIME: 15 MIN

COOKING TIME: 10 MIN

SERVINGS: 4

GRILLED SQUID SALAD WITH LEMON AND OLIVE OIL

Ingredients

- 1 lb. squid, cleaned and sliced
- 2 tablespoons olive oil
- 2 cloves garlic, minced
- Zest and juice of 1 lemon
- Salt and black pepper to taste
- 4 cups mixed salad greens
- 1 cup cherry tomatoes, halved
- 1/4 cup Kalamata olives, pitted and halved
- 2 tablespoons chopped fresh parsley

Directions

1. Preheat the grill over high heat. Combine the two tbsp olive oil, minced garlic, lemon zest, lemon juice, salt, and crushed pepper in a bowl. Add the squid rings and toss to coat. Grill the squid rings for 2-3 minutes for each side until cooked thoroughly.
2. Combine the mixed salad greens, cherry tomatoes, Kalamata olives, and chopped parsley in a salad bowl. Add grilled squid to the salad bowl and toss gently to combine. Serve the grilled squid salad immediately.

Nutritions

Calories: 180 , Fat: 8g , Protein: 22g , Carbohydrate: 7g

PREPARATION TIME: 20 MIN

COOKING TIME: 5 MIN

SERVINGS: 4

BAKED TROUT WITH LEMON AND THYME

Ingredients

- 4 trout fillets
- 2 tablespoons olive oil
- Zest and juice of 1 lemon
- 2 teaspoons chopped fresh thyme
- Salt and black pepper to taste
- Lemon wedges for serving

Directions

1. Set the oven heat to 400°F (200°C). Arrange the baking sheet with parchment paper. Put the trout fillets on the arranged baking sheet. Whisk the two tbsp olive oil with lemon zest, lemon juice, chopped thyme, salt, and crushed pepper in a bowl.
2. Stir well to combine. Drizzle the lemon and thyme mixture over the trout fillets, spreading it evenly. Bake for 17-20 minutes until cooked thoroughly.
3. Serve the baked trout with lemon wedges.

Nutritions

Calories: 250 , Fat: 12g , Protein: 30g , Carbohydrate: 2g

PREPARATION TIME: 10 MIN

COOKING TIME: 20 MIN

SERVINGS: 4

SHRIMP AND COUSCOUS WITH FETA

Ingredients

- 1 lb. shrimp, peeled and deveined
- 1 tablespoon olive oil
- 2 cloves garlic, minced
- 1 teaspoon ground cumin
- 1/2 teaspoon smoked paprika
- Salt and black pepper to taste
- 1 cup whole wheat couscous
- 1 cup vegetable broth
- 1 cup diced cucumber
- 1 cup diced tomatoes
- 1/2 cup crumbled feta cheese
- 2 tablespoons chopped fresh parsley
- Lemon wedges for serving

Directions

1. In a skillet, heat one tbsp of oil over medium heat. Add smashed garlic and sauté for one minute, until fragrant. Add shrimp and sprinkle with ground cumin, smoked paprika, salt, and crushed pepper.
2. Cook the shrimp for 2-3 minutes for each side or until pink and cooked. Remove the shrimp and set aside. In the same skillet, add the couscous and vegetable broth.
3. Take a boil, decrease the stove heat to low, cover, and simmer for 5 minutes. Fluff the cooked couscous, then transfer it to a large serving bowl. Add cooked shrimp, diced cucumber, tomatoes, crumbled feta cheese, and chopped parsley to the bowl. Toss gently to combine. Serve the shrimp and couscous salad with lemon wedges.

Nutritions

Calories: 350 , Fat: 8g , Protein: 30g , Carbohydrate: 40g

PREPARATION TIME: 15 MIN

COOKING TIME: 10 MIN

SERVINGS: 4

GRILLED SCALLOPS WITH GARLIC AND HERBS

Ingredients

- 1 lb scallops
- 2 tablespoons olive oil
- 2 cloves garlic, minced
- 1 teaspoon chopped fresh thyme
- 1 teaspoon chopped fresh rosemary
- Salt and black pepper to taste
- Lemon wedges for serving

Directions

1. Preheat the grill over high heat. Whisk the two tbsp oil with minced garlic, chopped thyme, chopped rosemary, salt, and black pepper in a bowl. Stir well to combine. Add the scallops to the bowl and toss to coat with the garlic and herb mixture.
2. Grill the scallops for 2-3 minutes for each side until cooked thoroughly. Serve the grilled scallops with lemon wedges.

Nutritions

Calories: 150 , Fat: 6g , Protein: 20g , Carbohydrate: 1g

PREPARATION TIME: 10 MIN

COOKING TIME: 5 MIN

SERVINGS: 4

MEDITERRANEAN FISH STEW WITH GARLIC AND SAFFRON

Ingredients

- 1 lb white fish fillets (cod or halibut or any other) cut into chunks
- 1 lb shrimp, peeled and deveined
- 2 tablespoons olive oil
- 1 onion, diced
- 3 cloves garlic, minced
- 1 red bell pepper, diced
- 1 can (14 oz) diced tomatoes
- 2 cups vegetable broth
- 1/2 teaspoon saffron threads
- 1 teaspoon dried oregano
- Salt and black pepper to taste
- 2 tablespoons chopped fresh parsley
- Lemon wedges for serving

Directions

1. In a non-stick stockpot, heat two tbsp oil over medium heat. Add diced onion and minced garlic. Sauté for 2-3 minutes until the onion becomes translucent. Add diced bell pepper and cook for 2 minutes.
2. Add diced tomatoes, vegetable broth, saffron threads, dried oregano, salt, and black pepper. Take this mixture to a boil, then decrease the stove heat to low and simmer for 10 minutes.
3. Add fish fillets and shrimp and cook for 5-7 minutes until the seafood is done properly. Stir in the chopped parsley. Serve the Mediterranean fish stew in bowls with lemon wedges on the side.

Nutritions

Calories: 250 , Fat: 8g , Protein: 30g , Carbohydrate: 12g

PREPARATION TIME: 15 MIN

COOKING TIME: 25 MIN

SERVINGS: 4

BAKED HADDOCK WITH OLIVES AND TOMATOES

Ingredients

- 4 haddock fillets
- 2 tablespoons olive oil
- 2 cloves garlic, minced
- 1 cup cherry tomatoes, halved
- 1/4 cup Kalamata olives, pitted and halved
- 1 tablespoon chopped fresh parsley
- Salt and black pepper to taste
- Lemon wedges for serving

Directions

1. Set the oven heat to 400°F (200°C). Arrange the baking sheet with parchment paper. Place the haddock fillets on the prepared baking. Whisk two tbsp oil, minced garlic, cherry tomatoes, Kalamata olives, chopped parsley, salt, and crushed in a bowl pepper. Stir well to combine.
2. Spoon the olive and tomato mixture over the haddock fillets, spreading it evenly. Bake for 12-15 minutes until it is done and flakes easily. Serve the baked haddock with lemon wedges.

Nutritions

Calories: 180 , Fat: 8g , Protein: 25g , Carbohydrate: 4g

PREPARATION TIME: 10 MIN

COOKING TIME: 15 MIN

SERVINGS: 4

GRILLED TUNA STEAKS WITH CAPER VINAIGRETTE

Ingredients

- 4 tuna steaks
- 2 tablespoons olive oil
- 2 tablespoons lemon juice
- 1 tablespoon capers, drained and chopped
- 1 tablespoon chopped fresh parsley
- 1 clove garlic, minced
- Salt and black pepper to taste

Directions

1. Burn the grill or preheat the grill pan over high heat. Whisk; whisk the olive oil with lemon juice, chopped capers, chopped parsley, minced garlic, salt, and crushed pepper to make the vinaigrette.
2. Season the tuna steaks with salt and crushed pepper. Grill the tuna steaks for 2-3 minutes for each side. Drizzle the caper vinaigrette over the grilled tuna steaks. Serve the tuna steaks with your choice of side dishes.

Nutritions

Calories: 200 , Fat: 8g , Protein: 30g , Carbohydrate: 1g

PREPARATION TIME: 10 MIN

COOKING TIME: 6 MIN

SERVINGS: 4

MEDITERRANEAN SHRIMP AND VEGETABLE SKEWERS

Ingredients

- 1 lb large shrimp, peeled and deveined
- 1 zucchini, sliced
- 1 yellow bell pepper, diced
- 1 red onion, diced
- 2 tablespoons olive oil
- 1 tablespoon lemon juice
- 2 cloves garlic, minced
- 1 teaspoon dried oregano
- Salt and black pepper to taste

Directions

1. Fire the grill or preheat the grilled pan over medium-highWhisk; whisk the two tbsp oil with lemon juice, minced garlic, dried oregano, salt, and black in a bowl pepper. Stir well to combine.
2. Thread the shrimp, zucchini slices, yellow bell pepper, and red onion onto skewers. Brush each skewer with the oil mixture, coating all sides. Grill the shrimp and vegetable skewers for 3-4 minutes for each side.
3. Serve the Mediterranean shrimp and vegetable skewers with your choice of side dishes.

Nutritions

Calories: 180 , Fat: 6g , Protein: 25g , Carbohydrate: 8g

PREPARATION TIME: 15 MIN

COOKING TIME: 10 MIN

SERVINGS: 4

SEAFOOD RISOTTO WITH SAFFRON

Ingredients

- 1 cup Arborio rice
- 4 cups vegetable broth
- ½ cup dry white wine
- 1 lb. mixed seafood (such as shrimp, scallops, and mussels)
- 1 onion, diced
- 2 cloves garlic, minced
- 2 tablespoons olive oil
- 1/4 teaspoon saffron threads
- Salt and black pepper to taste
- 2 tablespoons chopped fresh parsley
- Lemon wedges for serving

Directions

1. In the non-stick stockpot, heat two tbsp olive oil over medium heat. Add diced onion and minced garlic. Sauté for 2-3 minutes until the onion becomes translucent. Add Arborio rice and stir to coat the rice in the olive oil.
2. In the other pan, heat the vegetable broth and keep it warm over low heat. Add dry white wine to the pot with the rice and cook until the liquid is absorbed, stirring constantly.
3. Gradually add the warm vegetable broth to the rice, about ½ cup at a time, stirring regularly and allowing the liquid to be absorbed. Stir in the saffron threads and continue adding the vegetable broth and stirring until the rice is creamy and cooked al dente.
4. Meanwhile, in the other non-stick skillet, heat a bit of olive oil over medium heat. Add seafood and cook until done thoroughly. Once done, stir in the cooked seafood and chopped parsley.
5. Powder with salt and crushed pepper to taste. Serve the seafood risotto with lemon wedges on the side.

Nutritions

Calories: 350 , Fat: 6g , Protein: 25g , Carbohydrate: 45g

PREPARATION TIME: 15 MIN

COOKING TIME: 30 MIN

SERVINGS: 4

Chapter 6:

20 Mediterranean Beans and Cereals Recipes

GREEK LENTIL SOUP (FAKES)

Ingredients

- 1 cup dried lentils
- 1 onion, chopped
- 2 carrots, diced
- 2 celery stalks, diced
- 3 cloves garlic, minced
- 2 tablespoons olive oil
- 1 can diced tomatoes
- 4 cups vegetable broth
- 1 teaspoon dried oregano
- Salt and black pepper to taste
- Fresh lemon juice (optional)
- Fresh parsley for garnish

Directions

1. Rinse the lentils under water and set aside. In a non-stick stockpot, heat two tbsp oil over medium heat. Add chopped onion, carrots, celery, and minced garlic. Sauté until the vegetables are softened.
2. Add lentils with diced tomatoes, vegetable broth, dried oregano, salt, and crushed pepper to the pot. Take boil, then decrease the stove heat and simmer for 27-30 minutes, or until the lentils are tender.
3. Taste and adjust the seasoning as needed. Squeeze fresh lemon juice over the soup, if desired.
4. Serve the Greek lentil soup hot, garnished with fresh parsley.

Nutritions

Calories: 250 , Fat: 6g , Protein: 15g , Carbohydrate: 35g

PREPARATION TIME: 10 MIN

COOKING TIME: 40 MIN

SERVINGS:4

GREEK-STYLE GIGANTES PLAKI (BAKED GIANT BEANS)

Ingredients

- 2 cups dried giant white beans
- 1 onion, chopped
- 3 cloves garlic, minced
- 2 carrots, diced
- 2 celery stalks, diced
- 1 can diced tomatoes
- 1/4 cup tomato paste
- 1 tablespoon dried oregano
- 1 tablespoon dried thyme
- 1 teaspoon ground cumin
- Salt and black pepper to taste
- 2 tablespoons olive oil
- Fresh parsley for garnish

Directions

1. Soak the dried giant white beans in water overnight. Drain and rinse the beans.
2. In a non-stick stockpot, cover the beans with water and take a boil. Cook for 15 minutes, then drain.
3. In the same pot, heat two tbsp olive oil over medium heat. Add onion, minced garlic, diced carrots, and diced celery. Sauté until the vegetables are softened.
4. Add cooked beans, diced tomatoes, tomato paste, dried oregano, dried thyme, ground cumin, salt, and crushed pepper to the pot. Stir well to combine.
5. Cover and simmer over low heat for one hour or until the beans are tender and the flavors are well blended.
6. Adjust the seasoning if needed.
7. Serve the Greek-style gigantes place hot, garnished with fresh parsley.

Nutritions

Calories: 300 , Fat: 4g , Protein: 15g , Carbohydrate: 55g

PREPARATION TIME: 15 MIN

COOKING TIME: 1 HR 30 MIN

SERVINGS: 6

GREEK BAKED BEANS WITH HONEY AND DILL

Ingredients

- 2 cups dried white beans
- 1 onion, chopped
- 3 cloves garlic, minced
- 2 carrots, diced
- 2 celery stalks, diced
- 1 can diced tomatoes
- ¼ cup tomato paste
- 2 tablespoons honey
- 2 tablespoons chopped fresh dill
- Salt and black pepper to taste
- 2 tablespoons olive oil

Directions

1. Soak the dried white beans in water overnight. Drain and rinse the beans. In the non-stick stockpot, cover the beans with water and take a boil. Cook for 15 minutes, then drain.
2. In the non-stick stockpot, heat two tbsp oil over medium heat. Add onion with minced garlic, diced carrots, and diced celery. Sauté until the vegetables are softened.
3. Add prepared beans, diced tomatoes, tomato paste, honey, chopped fresh dill, salt, and crushed pepper to the pot. Stir well to combine.
4. Cover and simmer for one hour over low flame until the beans are tender and the flavors are well blended. Adjust the seasoning if needed.
5. Serve the Greek baked beans hot.

Nutritions

Calories: 280 , Fat: 4g , Protein: 15g , Carbohydrate: 50g

PREPARATION TIME: 10 MIN

COOKING TIME: 1 HR 30 MIN

SERVINGS: 6

BULGUR AND LENTIL SALAD

Ingredients

- 1 cup bulgur wheat
- 1 cup cooked lentils
- 1 cucumber, diced
- 1 tomato, diced
- 1/4 cup chopped fresh parsley
- 1/4 cup chopped fresh mint
- 2 tablespoons lemon juice
- 2 tablespoons olive oil
- Salt and black pepper to taste

Directions

1. Cook the bulgur wheat as directed by package instructions. Let it cool. Combine the cooked lentils with diced cucumber, tomato, chopped fresh parsley, chopped fresh mint, lemon juice, olive oil, salt, and crushed pepper in a bowl. Mix well.
2. Add prepared bulgur wheat to the bowl and toss everything together until well combined.
3. Adjust the seasoning if needed.
4. Serve the Mediterranean bulgur and lentil salad at room temperature or chilled.

Nutritions

Calories: 250 , Fat: 6g , Protein: 12g , Carbohydrate: 40g

PREPARATION TIME: 15 MIN

COOKING TIME: 25 MIN

SERVINGS: 4

GREEK-STYLE LENTIL AND SPINACH SOUP

Ingredients

- 1 cup dried green lentils
- 1 onion, chopped
- 3 cloves garlic, minced
- 2 carrots, diced
- 2 celery stalks, diced
- 4 cups vegetable broth
- 1 can diced tomatoes
- 2 cups chopped fresh spinach
- Juice of 1 lemon
- Salt and black pepper to taste
- 2 tablespoons olive oil

Directions

1. Rinse the dried green lentils under water and set aside. In the deep-bottom pot, heat two tbsp oil over medium heat. Add onion with minced garlic, diced carrots, and diced celery. Sauté until the vegetables are softened.
2. Add rinsed lentils, vegetable broth, and diced tomatoes to the pot. Bring to a boil, then decrease the stove heat and simmer for 23-25 minutes or until the lentils are tender.
3. Stir in the chopped fresh spinach and cook for five minutes or until the spinach wilts.
4. Remove the pot and add lemon juice. Powder the dish with salt and crushed pepper to taste. Serve the Greek-style lentil and spinach soup hot.

Nutritions

Calories: 280 , Fat: 6g , Protein: 15g , Carbohydrate: 45g

PREPARATION TIME: 10 MIN

COOKING TIME: 30 MIN

SERVINGS: 4

GREEK FAVA (YELLOW SPLIT PEA PUREE)

Ingredients

- 1 cup yellow split peas
- 1 onion, chopped
- 3 cloves garlic, minced
- 2 carrots, diced
- 2 celery stalks, diced
- 4 cups vegetable broth
- Juice of 1 lemon
- Salt and black pepper to taste
- 2 tablespoons olive oil

Directions

1. Rinse the yellow split peas under water and set aside. In the non-stick stockpot, heat two tbsp oil over medium heat. Add chopped onion with minced garlic, diced carrots, and diced celery. Sauté until the vegetables are softened.
2. Add rinsed split peas and vegetable broth to the pot. Take a boil, then decrease the stove heat and simmer for 41-45 minutes until the peas are tender.
3. Use the food blender to puree the cooked split peas until smooth. Add pureed mixture to the stockpot and heat over low heat. Stir in the lemon juice, salt, and black pepper. Adjust the seasoning if needed.
4. Serve the Greek Fava hot, drizzled with a little olive oil.

Nutritions

Calories: 230 , Fat: 6g , Protein: 12g , Carbohydrate: 35g

PREPARATION TIME: 10 MIN

COOKING TIME: 45 MIN

SERVINGS: 4

GREEK-STYLE BAKED LIMA BEANS (GIGANDES)

Ingredients

- 2 cups dried lima beans
- 1 onion, chopped
- 4 cloves garlic, minced
- 1 carrot, diced
- 1 celery stalk, diced
- 1 can diced tomatoes
- 1/4 cup tomato paste
- 2 tablespoons olive oil
- 1 tablespoon dried oregano
- 1 bay leaf
- Salt and black pepper to taste

Directions

1. Place the dried lima beans in a bowl and cover with water. Allow them to soak for 8 hours. Drain and rinse the beans. Set the oven heat to 350°F (175°C).
2. In the oven-safe pot, heat two tbsp oil over medium heat. Add onion with minced garlic, diced carrot, and diced celery. Sauté until the vegetables are softened.
3. Add the soaked and drained lima beans with diced tomatoes, tomato paste, dried oregano, bay leaf, salt, and crushed pepper to the pot. Stir well to combine.
4. Cover the pot and shift it to the preheated oven. Bake for one hour and 30 minutes until the beans are tender. Remove the pot from the oven and discard the bay leaf.

Nutritions

Calories: 280 , Fat: 4g , Protein: 14g , Carbohydrate: 50g

PREPARATION TIME: 8 HR

COOKING TIME: 1 HR 30 MIN

SERVINGS: 6

BUCKWHEAT SALAD WITH LEMON AND OLIVES

Ingredients

- 1 cup buckwheat groats
- 2 cups vegetable broth
- 1 cucumber, diced
- 1 tomato, diced
- 1/4 cup sliced Kalamata olives
- 2 tablespoons chopped fresh parsley
- 2 tablespoons chopped fresh mint
- Juice of 1 lemon
- 2 tablespoons extra-virgin olive oil
- Salt and black pepper to taste

Directions

1. Rinse the buckwheat groats under cold water. In a saucepan, add vegetable broth to a boil. Add the rinsed buckwheat groats, take a boil, then reduce heat to low. Cover and simmer for 17-20 minutes.
2. Remove the cooked buckwheat from the heat and let it cool. Combine the cooled buckwheat, diced cucumber, tomato, sliced Kalamata olives, chopped parsley, and chopped mint
3. in a large bowl.
4. Whisk the lemon juice with olive oil, salt, and crushed pepper in a bowl. Pour the lemon oil dressing over the salad ingredients and toss to coat evenly. Adjust the seasoning if needed. Serve the Mediterranean Buckwheat Salad chilled or at room temperature.

Nutritions

Calories: 220 , Fat: 9g , Protein: 6g , Carbohydrate: 30g

PREPARATION TIME: 15 MIN

COOKING TIME: 20 MIN

SERVINGS: 4

MILLET SALAD WITH SUN-DRIED TOMATOES

Ingredients

- 1 cup millet
- 2 cups vegetable broth
- 1/4 cup chopped sun-dried tomatoes
- 1/4 cup sliced Kalamata olives
- 2 tablespoons chopped fresh parsley
- 2 tablespoons chopped fresh basil
- Juice of 1 lemon
- 2 tablespoons extra-virgin olive oil
- Salt and black pepper to taste

Directions

1. Rinse the millet under cold water. In a saucepan, add vegetable broth to a boil. Add rinsed millet and reduce heat to low. Cover and simmer for 17-20 minutes. Remove the cooked millet from the heat and let it cool.
2. Combine the cooled millet with chopped sun-dried tomatoes, sliced Kalamata olives, chopped parsley, and chopped basil in a bowl. Whisk the lemon juice with olive oil, salt, and crushed pepper in a bowl.
3. Pour the lemon oil dressing over the salad ingredients and toss to coat evenly. Adjust the seasoning if needed. Serve the Mediterranean Millet Salad chilled or at room temperature.

Nutritions

Calories: 250 , Fat: 10g , Protein: 7g , Carbohydrate: 33g

PREPARATION TIME: 10 MIN

COOKING TIME: 20 MIN

SERVINGS: 4

GREEK-STYLE BAKED CHICKPEAS WITH TOMATO

Ingredients

- 2 cups dried chickpeas
- 1 onion, chopped
- 4 cloves garlic, minced
- 1 carrot, diced
- 1 celery stalk, diced
- 1 can diced tomatoes
- 1/4 cup tomato paste
- 2 tablespoons olive oil
- 2 teaspoons dried oregano
- 1 bay leaf
- Salt and black pepper to taste

Directions

1. Put the dried chickpeas in the bowl and cover with water. Allow them to soak overnight or for at least 8 hours. Drain and rinse the chickpeas. Set the oven heat to 350°F (175°C).
2. Heat two tbsp oil over medium heat in a large oven-safe pot or Dutch oven. Add the chopped onion, minced garlic, carrot, and celery. Sauté until the vegetables are softened.
3. Add the soaked and drained chickpeas, diced tomatoes, tomato paste, dried oregano, bay leaf, salt, and black pepper to the pot. Stir well to combine.
4. Cover and shift it to the preheated oven. Bake for one hour and thirty minutes until the chickpeas are tender and the flavors are well blended.
5. Remove the pot from the oven and discard the bay leaf.
6. Serve the Greek-Style Baked Chickpeas hot.

Nutritions

Calories: 280 , Fat: 5g , Protein: 13g , Carbohydrate: 47g

PREPARATION TIME: 8 HR

COOKING TIME: 1 HR 30 MIN

SERVINGS: 6

COUSCOUS AND LENTIL SALAD

Ingredients

- 1 cup couscous
- 1 cup cooked lentils
- 1 cucumber, diced
- 1 tomato, diced
- 1/4 cup chopped fresh parsley
- 1/4 cup chopped fresh mint
- Juice of 1 lemon
- 2 tablespoons extra-virgin olive oil
- Salt and black pepper to taste

Directions

1. Prepare the couscous as directed by package instructions. Fluff it and let it cool.
2. Whisk the cooked couscous, lentils, cucumber, tomato, chopped parsley, and chopped mint
3. in a bowl.
4. Whisk the lemon juice with olive oil, salt, and black pepper in a small bowl. Pour the lemon oil dressing over the salad ingredients and toss to coat evenly.
5. Adjust the seasoning if needed. Serve the Mediterranean Couscous and Lentil Salad chilled or at room temperature.

Nutritions

Calories: 280 , Fat: 6g , Protein: 12g , Carbohydrate: 46g

PREPARATION TIME: 15 MIN

COOKING TIME: 15 MIN

SERVINGS: 4

BARLEY AND CHICKPEA SOUP

Ingredients

- 1 cup pearl barley
- 1 can chickpeas, drained and rinsed
- 1 onion, chopped
- 2 carrots, diced
- 2 celery stalks, diced
- 4 cloves garlic, minced
- 6 cups vegetable broth
- 1 teaspoon dried thyme
- 1 teaspoon dried oregano
- Salt and black pepper to taste
- Fresh parsley, chopped (for garnish)

Directions

1. In a non-stick stockpot, heat some olive oil over medium heat. Add onion with diced carrots, diced celery, and minced garlic. Sauté until the vegetables are softened.
2. Add the pearl barley, chickpeas, vegetable broth, dried thyme, oregano, salt, and crushed pepper to the pot. Stir well to combine.
3. Take this mixture to a boil, then decrease the stove heat to low. Cover the pot and simmer for 41-45 minutes or until the barley is tender.
4. Adjust seasoning if needed. Serve the Mediterranean Barley and Chickpea Soup hot, garnished with fresh chopped parsley.

Nutritions

Calories: 220 , Fat: 2g , Protein: 9g , Carbohydrate: 44g

PREPARATION TIME: 10 MIN

COOKING TIME: 45 MIN

SERVINGS: 6

GREEK-STYLE BLACK EYED PEAS SALAD

Ingredients

- 1 cup dried black-eyed peas
- 1 onion, chopped
- 2 cloves garlic, minced
- 1 red bell pepper, diced
- 1 cucumber, diced
- 1/4 cup sliced Kalamata olives
- 2 tablespoons chopped fresh parsley
- 2 tablespoons chopped fresh dill
- Juice of 1 lemon
- 2 tablespoons extra-virgin olive oil
- Salt and black pepper to taste

Directions

1. Place the dried black-eyed peas in a bowl and cover with water. Soak them for 6 hours or overnight. Drain and rinse the black-eyed peas.
2. In the non-stick stockpot, take the water to a boil, then add the soaked black-eyed peas. Cook for about 47-50 minutes or until tender. Drain and let them cool.
3. Combine the cooked black-eyed peas with onion, minced garlic, red bell pepper, cucumber, sliced Kalamata olives, chopped parsley, and chopped dill.
4. Whisk the lemon juice with olive oil, salt, and crushed pepper in a bowl. Pour the lemon oil dressing over the salad ingredients and toss to coat evenly.
5. Adjust the seasoning if needed. Serve the Greek-Style Black Eyed Peas Salad chilled or at room temperature.

Nutritions

Calories: 210 , Fat: 7g , Protein: 8g , Carbohydrate: 30g

PREPARATION TIME: 10 MIN

COOKING TIME: 50 MIN

SERVINGS: 4

BULGUR AND RED LENTIL SOUP

Ingredients

- ½ cup bulgur wheat
- ½ cup red lentils
- 1 onion, chopped
- 2 carrots, diced
- 2 celery stalks, diced
- 4 cloves garlic, minced
- 6 cups vegetable broth
- 1 teaspoon ground cumin
- 1 teaspoon paprika
- Salt and black pepper to taste
- Fresh parsley, chopped (for garnish)

Directions

1. In the non-stick stockpot, heat some olive oil over medium heat. Add onion with diced carrots, diced celery, and minced garlic. Sauté until the vegetables are softened.
2. Add the bulgur wheat, red lentils, vegetable broth, ground cumin, paprika, salt, and crushed pepper to the pot. Stir well to combine.
3. Take this mixture to a boil, then decrease the stove heat to low. Cover the pot and simmer for about 27-30 minutes.
4. Adjust the seasoning if needed. Serve the Mediterranean Bulgur and Red Lentil Soup hot, garnished with fresh chopped parsley.

Nutritions

Calories: 260 , Fat: 1g , Protein: 12g , Carbohydrate: 50g

PREPARATION TIME: 10 MIN

COOKING TIME: 30 MIN

SERVINGS: 4

GREEK-STYLE BROWN RICE AND LENTIL SOUP

Ingredients

- 1/2 cup brown lentils
- 1/2 cup brown rice
- 1 onion, chopped
- 2 carrots, diced
- 2 celery stalks, diced
- 4 cloves garlic, minced
- 6 cups vegetable broth
- 1 teaspoon dried oregano
- 1 teaspoon dried thyme
- Salt and black pepper to taste
- Fresh lemon juice (for serving)

Directions

1. In the non-stick stockpot, heat some olive oil over medium heat. Add onion with diced carrots, diced celery, and minced garlic. Sauté until the vegetables are softened.
2. Add brown lentils, brown rice, vegetable broth, dried oregano, dried thyme, salt, and crushed pepper to the pot. Stir well to combine.
3. Take this mixture to a boil, then decrease the stove heat to low. Cover the pot and simmer for about 37-40 minutes.
4. Adjust the seasoning if needed. Serve the hot Greek-Style Brown Rice and Lentil Soup, squeezing fresh lemon juice over each serving.

Nutritions

Calories: 240 , Fat: 1g , Protein: 10g , Carbohydrate: 50g

PREPARATION TIME: 10 MIN

COOKING TIME: 40 MIN

SERVINGS: 4

QUINOA AND WHITE BEAN STEW

Ingredients

- 1 cup quinoa
- 1 can white beans, drained and rinsed
- 1 onion, chopped
- 2 carrots, diced
- 2 celery stalks, diced
- 4 cloves garlic, minced
- 6 cups vegetable broth
- 1 teaspoon dried rosemary
- 1 teaspoon dried thyme
- Salt and black pepper to taste
- Fresh parsley, chopped (for garnish)

Directions

1. In the non-stick stockpot, heat some olive oil over medium heat. Add onion with diced carrots, diced celery, and minced garlic. Sauté until the vegetables are softened.
2. Add the quinoa, white beans, vegetable broth, dried rosemary, dried thyme, salt, and crushed pepper to the pot. Stir well to combine.
3. Take this mixture to a boil, then decrease the stove heat to low. Cover and simmer for 23-25 minutes until the quinoa is cooked and the stew thickens.
4. Adjust the seasoning if needed. Serve the hot Quinoa and White Bean Stew, garnished with fresh chopped parsley.

Nutritions

Calories: 290 , Fat: 3g , Protein: 13g , Carbohydrate: 54g

PREPARATION TIME: 10 MIN

COOKING TIME: 30 MIN

SERVINGS: 4

GREEK-STYLE LENTIL AND TOMATO STEW

Ingredients

- 1 cup green lentils
- 1 onion, chopped
- 2 carrots, diced
- 2 celery stalks, diced
- 4 cloves garlic, minced
- 1 can diced tomatoes
- 4 cups vegetable broth
- 1 teaspoon dried oregano
- 1 teaspoon dried basil
- Salt and black pepper to taste
- Fresh parsley, chopped (for garnish)

Directions

1. In the non-stick stockpot, heat some olive oil over medium heat. Add onion, diced carrots, diced celery, and minced garlic. Sauté until the vegetables are softened.
2. Add green lentils, diced tomatoes (with juices), vegetable broth, dried oregano, dried basil, salt, and black pepper to the pot. Stir well to combine.
3. Take this mixture to a boil, then decrease stove the heat to low. Cover and simmer for 33-35 minutes until the lentils are tender.
4. Adjust the seasoning if needed. Top with parsley

Nutritions

Calories: 240 , Fat: 1g , Protein: 14g , Carbohydrate: 48g

PREPARATION TIME: 10 MIN

COOKING TIME: 40 MIN

SERVINGS: 4

QUINOA AND CANNELLINI BEAN SALAD

Ingredients

- 1 cup quinoa
- 1 can cannellini beans, drained and rinsed
- 1 cucumber, diced
- 1 tomato, diced
- 1/4 cup sliced Kalamata olives
- 2 tablespoons chopped fresh parsley
- 2 tablespoons chopped fresh mint
- Juice of 1 lemon
- 2 tablespoons extra-virgin olive oil
- Salt and black pepper to taste

Directions

1. Prepare the quinoa as directed by package instructions. Fluff it and let it cool.
2. Combine the cooked quinoa, cannellini beans, cucumber, tomato, sliced Kalamata olives, parsley, and mint
3. in a bowl.
4. Whisk the lemon juice with olive oil, salt, and crushed pepper in a bowl. Pour the lemon oil dressing over the salad ingredients and toss to coat evenly.
5. Adjust the seasoning if needed. Serve the Quinoa and Cannellini Bean Salad chilled or at room temperature.

Nutritions

Calories: 280 , Fat: 6g , Protein: 12g , Carbohydrate: 46g

PREPARATION TIME: 15 MIN

COOKING TIME: 15 MIN

SERVINGS: 4

GREEK CHICKPEA AND SPINACH STEW

Ingredients

- 2 cans chickpeas, drained and rinsed
- 1 onion, chopped
- 4 cloves garlic, minced
- 1 teaspoon ground cumin
- 1 teaspoon ground coriander
- ½ teaspoon paprika
- 4 cups vegetable broth
- 4 cups fresh spinach leaves
- Juice of 1 lemon
- Salt and black pepper to taste

Directions

1. In a non-stick stockpot, heat some olive oil over medium heat. Add diced onion with smashed garlic. Sauté until the onion is softened.
2. Add ground cumin, ground coriander, and paprika to the pot. Stir well to coat the onions and garlic with the spices.
3. Add chickpeas and vegetable broth to the pot. Take this mixture to a simmer and cook for 17-20 minutes.
4. Add fresh spinach leaves and cook for 3-5 minutes or until the spinach is wilted.
5. Remove the pot and whisk lemon juice. Powder the dish with salt and crushed pepper to taste.
6. Adjust the seasoning if needed. Serve the Chickpea and Spinach Stew with Lemon hot.

Nutritions

Calories: 250 , Fat: 3g , Protein: 11g , Carbohydrate: 46g

PREPARATION TIME: 10 MIN

COOKING TIME: 30 MIN

SERVINGS: 4

BARLEY AND LENTIL SOUP WITH SPINACH

Ingredients

- 1/2 cup barley
- 1/2 cup green lentils
- 1 onion, chopped
- 2 carrots, diced
- 2 celery stalks, diced
- 4 cloves garlic, minced
- 6 cups vegetable broth
- 2 cups fresh spinach leaves
- 1 teaspoon dried thyme
- 1 teaspoon dried rosemary
- Salt and black pepper to taste

Directions

1. In the non-stick stockpot, heat some olive oil over medium heat. Add diced onion with diced carrots, diced celery, and minced garlic. Sauté until the vegetables are softened.
2. Add barley, green lentils, vegetable broth, dried thyme, rosemary, salt, and crushed pepper to the pot. Stir well to combine.
3. Take the mixture to a boil, then decrease the stove heat to low. Cover and simmer for 33-35 minutes or until the barley and lentils are tender.
4. Add spinach leaves and cook for 5 minutes until it is wilted.
5. Adjust the seasoning if needed. Serve the Barley and Lentil Soup with Spinach hot.

Nutritions

Calories: 240 , Fat: 1g , Protein: 10g , Carbohydrate: 50g

PREPARATION TIME: 10 MIN

COOKING TIME: 40 MIN

SERVINGS: 4

Chapter 7:

20 Mediterranean Pasta Recipes

MEDITERRANEAN SPAGHETTI WITH GARLIC AND OLIVE OIL

Ingredients

- 8 ounces whole wheat spaghetti
- 4 tablespoons extra-virgin olive oil
- 4 cloves garlic, minced
- 1/4 teaspoon red pepper flakes (optional)
- Salt and black pepper to taste
- Fresh parsley, chopped (for garnish)

Directions

1. Prepare the spaghetti as directed by package instructions until al dente. Drain and set aside. In a non-stick skillet, heat 4 tbsp oil over medium heat. Add minced garlic with red pepper flakes (if using). Sauté for about 1 minute until the garlic is fragrant and lightly golden.
2. Add prepared spaghetti and toss well to coat the pasta with the garlic-infused olive oil. Powder with salt and crushed pepper to taste. Serve the Spaghetti with Garlic and Olive Oil hot and top with fresh chopped parsley.

Nutritions

Calories: 280 , Fat: 14g , Protein: 7g , Carbohydrate: 35g

PREPARATION TIME: 10 MIN

COOKING TIME: 15 MIN

SERVINGS: 4

GREEK PASTA SALAD WITH FETA AND OLIVES

Ingredients

- 8 ounces whole wheat rotini pasta
- 1 cucumber, diced
- 1 bell pepper, diced
- 1 cup cherry tomatoes, halved
- 1/4 cup Kalamata olives, pitted and sliced
- 2 tablespoons red onion, finely chopped
- 4 ounces feta cheese, crumbled
- 2 tablespoons extra-virgin olive oil
- 2 tablespoons lemon juice
- 1 teaspoon dried oregano
- Salt and black pepper to taste

Directions

1. Prepare the rotini pasta as directed by package instructions until al dente. Drain and let it cool.
2. Toss the cooled pasta, diced cucumber, bell pepper, cherry tomatoes, sliced Kalamata olives, and finely chopped red onion
3. in a bowl.
4. Whisk the olive oil with lemon juice, dried oregano, salt, and crushed pepper in a bowl. Pour the lemon oil dressing over the pasta salad ingredients and toss well to coat. Add crumbled feta cheese to the salad and gently toss to combine.
5. Adjust the seasoning if needed. Serve the Greek Pasta Salad with Feta and Olives at room temperature.

Nutritions

Calories: 350 , Fat: 12g , Protein: 12g , Carbohydrate: 50g

PREPARATION TIME: 15 MIN

COOKING TIME: 10 MIN

SERVINGS: 4

LINGUINE WITH CLAMS IN WHITE WINE SAUCE

Ingredients

- 8 ounces whole wheat linguine
- 2 pounds of clams, scrubbed and rinsed
- 4 tablespoons extra-virgin olive oil
- 4 cloves garlic, minced
- ½ cup dry white wine
- ¼ cup fresh parsley, chopped
- Salt and black pepper to taste

Directions

1. Prepare linguine as directed by package instructions until al dente. Set aside after draining. Warm the olive oil in a non-stick skillet over medium heat. Sauté the minced garlic for about 1 minute or until fragrant.
2. Pour the white wine
3. over the clams in the skillet.
4. Cover and cook for 6-7 minutes or until the clams open. Remove any clams that haven't been opened from the skillet. Powder the sauce to taste with salt and black pepper. Add prepared linguine to the skillet with the clams and sauce. Toss well to coat the pasta with the sauce.
5. Sprinkle with fresh chopped parsley. Serve the Linguine with Clams in White Wine Sauce hot.

Nutritions

Calories: 340 , Fat: 10g , Protein: 20g , Carbohydrate: 40g

PREPARATION TIME: 15 MIN

COOKING TIME: 15 MIN

SERVINGS: 4

WHOLE GRAIN PENNE WITH SUN-DRIED TOMATO PESTO

Ingredients

- 8 ounces whole grain penne pasta
- 1/2 cup sun-dried tomatoes (packed in oil), drained and chopped
- 2 tablespoons pine nuts
- 2 cloves garlic, minced
- 1/4 cup fresh basil leaves
- 1/4 cup grated Parmesan cheese
- 2 tablespoons extra-virgin olive oil
- Salt and black pepper to taste

Directions

1. Prepare penne pasta as directed by package instructions until al dente. Drain and set aside.
2. Combine sun-dried tomatoes, pine nuts, minced garlic, fresh basil leaves, grated Parmesan cheese, and extra-virgin olive oil in a food blender. Process until well combined and a thick pesto-like consistency is formed.
3. Toss the prepared penne pasta with the sun-dried tomato pesto until evenly coated. Powder with salt and crushed pepper to taste. Serve the Whole Grain Penne with Sun-Dried Tomato Pesto hot.

Nutritions

Calories: 380 , Fat: 12g , Protein: 12g , Carbohydrate: 55g

PREPARATION TIME: 10 MIN

COOKING TIME: 15 MIN

SERVINGS: 4

MEDITERRANEAN ORZO SALAD WITH LEMON VINAIGRETTE

Ingredients

- 1 cup whole wheat orzo pasta
- 1 cup cucumber, diced
- 1 cup cherry tomatoes, halved
- ½ cup Kalamata olives, pitted and halved
- ¼ cup red onion, finely chopped
- 2 tablespoons fresh parsley, chopped
- 2 tablespoons fresh mint, chopped
- 2 tablespoons extra-virgin olive oil
- 2 tablespoons lemon juice
- 1 teaspoon Dijon mustard
- Salt and black pepper to taste

Directions

1. Prepare orzo pasta as directed by package instructions until al dente. Drain and let it cool. In a bowl, combine the cooked orzo pasta, diced cucumber, halved cherry tomatoes, halved Kalamata olives, finely chopped red onion, chopped parsley, and chopped mint.
2. Whisk the olive oil with lemon juice, Dijon mustard, salt, and crushed pepper to make the lemon vinaigrette. Pour the lemon vinaigrette over the orzo salad ingredients and toss well to combine.
3. Adjust the seasoning if needed. Serve the Mediterranean Orzo Salad with Lemon Vinaigrette chilled or at room temperature.

Nutritions

Calories: 290 , Fat: 8g , Protein: 8g , Carbohydrate: 48g

PREPARATION TIME: 10 MIN

COOKING TIME: 10 MIN

SERVINGS: 4

SPAGHETTI WITH SHRIMP AND TOMATO SAUCE

Ingredients

- 8 ounces whole wheat spaghetti
- 1 pound shrimp, peeled and deveined
- 2 tablespoons extra-virgin olive oil
- 4 cloves garlic, minced
- 1 can (14 ounces) diced tomatoes, undrained
- 1 teaspoon dried oregano
- 1/2 teaspoon red pepper flakes (optional)
- Salt and black pepper to taste
- Fresh basil, chopped (for garnish)

Directions

1. Prepare spaghetti as directed by package instructions until al dente. Drain and set aside. Heat two tbsp oil in a non-stick skillet over medium heat. Sauté the minced garlic for about 1 minute or until fragrant.
2. Cook for 2-3 minutes for each side or until the prawns are pink and cooked. Take the prawns out of the skillet and leave aside.
3. Add diced tomatoes, dried oregano, red pepper flakes (if using), salt, and black pepper.
4. Stir well and simmer for about 10 minutes to allow the flavors to blend. Return the prepared shrimp to the skillet and toss to coat them with the tomato sauce. Serve the spaghetti topped with the shrimp and tomato sauce. Garnish with fresh chopped basil.

Nutritions

Calories: 320 , Fat: 8g , Protein: 25g , Carbohydrate: 36g

PREPARATION TIME: 10 MIN

COOKING TIME: 20 MIN

SERVINGS: 4

FETTUCCINE WITH MEDITERRANEAN VEGETABLE RAGOUT

Ingredients

- 8 ounces whole wheat fettuccine
- 2 tablespoons extra-virgin olive oil
- 1 onion, sliced
- 2 bell peppers, sliced
- 2 zucchini, sliced
- 2 cloves garlic, minced
- 1 can (14 ounces) diced tomatoes, undrained
- 1 teaspoon dried oregano
- Salt and black pepper to taste
- Fresh basil, chopped (for garnish)

Directions

1. Prepare fettuccine as directed by package instructions until al dente. Drain and set aside.
2. In a non-stick skillet, heat two tbsp oil over medium heat. Add the sliced onion and sauté for about 5 minutes until softened.
3. Add sliced bell peppers, zucchini, and minced garlic to the skillet. Cook for 5 minutes until the vegetables are tender-crisp. Pour the diced tomatoes with their juice and add the dried oregano, salt, and crushed pepper.
4. Stir well and simmer for about 10 minutes to allow the flavors to meld. Serve the cooked fettuccine topped with the Mediterranean vegetable ragout. Garnish with freshly chopped basil.

Nutritions

Calories: 290 , Fat: 8g , Protein: 10g , Carbohydrate: 46g

PREPARATION TIME: 15 MIN

COOKING TIME: 20 MIN

SERVINGS: 4

WHOLE GRAIN PASTA WITH EGGPLANT AND BASIL

Ingredients

- 8 ounces whole grain penne pasta
- 1 medium eggplant, diced
- 2 tablespoons extra-virgin olive oil
- 2 cloves garlic, minced
- 1 can (14 ounces) diced tomatoes, undrained
- 1/4 cup fresh basil leaves, chopped
- Salt and black pepper to taste
- Grated Parmesan cheese (optional for serving)

Directions

1. Prepare penne pasta as directed by package instructions until al dente. Drain and set aside.
2. In the non-stick skillet, heat two tbsp oil over medium heat. Add the diced eggplant and sauté for about 5 minutes until softened.
3. Add garlic and cook for a minute until fragrant. Add diced tomatoes with their juice and add the chopped basil, salt, and black pepper. Stir well and simmer for 9-10 minutes to allow the flavors to blend.
4. Add prepared penne pasta to the skillet and toss to coat it with the eggplant and tomato sauce.
5. Serve the pasta with eggplant and basil hot, and top with grated Parmesan cheese. Serve and enjoy.

Nutritions

Calories: 330 , Fat: 10g , Protein: 10g , Carbohydrate: 52g

PREPARATION TIME: 15 MIN

COOKING TIME: 25 MIN

SERVINGS: 4

FUSILLI WITH SPINACH AND GOAT CHEESE

Ingredients

- 8 ounces whole wheat fusilli pasta
- 2 tablespoons extra-virgin olive oil
- 4 cups fresh spinach leaves
- 2 cloves garlic, minced
- 1/4 teaspoon red pepper flakes (optional)
- 4 ounces goat cheese, crumbled
- Salt and black pepper to taste
- Lemon zest (for garnish)

Directions

1. Prepare fusilli pasta as directed by package instructions until al dente. Drain and set aside. In a non-stick skillet, heat two tbsp oil over medium heat. Add the fresh spinach leaves and sauté for 2-3 minutes until wilted.
2. Add smashed garlic with red pepper flakes to the skillet. Cook for another minute until the garlic is fragrant. Add cooked fusilli pasta to the skillet and toss it with the sautéed spinach and garlic.
3. Crumble the goat cheese over the pasta and gently toss to distribute it evenly. Powder with salt and crushed pepper to taste. Garnish with lemon zest. Serve the Fusilli with Spinach and Goat Cheese hot.

Nutritions

Calories: 380 , Fat: 12g , Protein: 14g , Carbohydrate: 55g

PREPARATION TIME: 10 MIN

COOKING TIME: 15 MIN

SERVINGS: 4

MEDITERRANEAN PASTA SALAD WITH TUNA AND CAPERS

Ingredients

- 8 ounces whole wheat rotini pasta
- 2 cans (5 ounces each) of tuna, drained
- 1/4 cup Kalamata olives, pitted and halved
- 2 tablespoons capers, drained
- 1/2 cup cherry tomatoes, halved
- 1/4 cup red onion, finely chopped
- 2 tablespoons fresh parsley, chopped
- 2 tablespoons extra-virgin olive oil
- 2 tablespoons lemon juice
- Salt and black pepper to taste

Directions

1. Prepare rotini pasta according to the package instructions until al dente. Drain and let it cool. Combine the cooked rotini pasta with drained tuna, halved Kalamata olives, drained capers, cherry tomatoes, finely chopped red onion, and chopped parsley
2. in a bowl.
3. Whisk the olive oil with lemon juice, salt, and crushed pepper in a small bowl to make the dressing.
4. Pour the lemon oil dressing over the pasta salad ingredients and toss well to combine. Adjust the seasoning if needed. Serve the Pasta Salad with Tuna and Capers chilled or at room temperature.

Nutritions

Calories: 350 , Fat: 10g , Protein: 20g , Carbohydrate: 45g

PREPARATION TIME: 10 MIN

COOKING TIME: 10 MIN

SERVINGS: 4

WHOLE GRAIN SPAGHETTI WITH GARLIC AND CHILIES

Ingredients

- 8 ounces whole grain spaghetti
- 3 tablespoons extra-virgin olive oil
- 4 cloves garlic, minced
- 1/2 teaspoon red pepper flakes
- 1/4 cup fresh parsley, chopped
- Salt and black pepper to taste
- Grated Parmesan cheese (optional for serving)

Directions

1. Prepare whole grain spaghetti as directed by package instructions until al dente. Drain and set aside. In a non-stick skillet, heat 3 tbsp olive oil over medium heat. Add minced garlic and red pepper flakes. Sauté for 1-2 minutes until the garlic is golden and fragrant.
2. Add prepared spaghetti to the skillet and toss it with the garlic and chili oil. Add chopped parsley and powder it with salt and black pepper to taste. Serve the Whole Grain Spaghetti with Garlic and Chilies hot, and sprinkle with grated Parmesan cheese if desired.

Nutritions

Calories: 300 , Fat: 10g , Protein: 8g , Carbohydrate: 45g

PREPARATION TIME: 10 MIN

COOKING TIME: 15 MIN

SERVINGS: 4

FARFALLE WITH PESTO, POTATOES, AND GREEN BEANS

Ingredients

- 8 ounces whole wheat farfalle pasta
- 2 cups baby potatoes, halved
- 1 cup green beans, trimmed and halved
- 1/4 cup pine nuts
- 2 cups fresh basil leaves
- 1/4 cup grated Parmesan cheese
- 2 cloves garlic, minced
- 1/4 cup extra-virgin olive oil
- Salt and black pepper to taste

Directions

1. Prepare farfalle pasta as directed by package instructions until al dente. Drain and set aside.
2. In the other pot, boil the baby potatoes for 10 minutes or until tender. Add green beans in the last 3 minutes of cooking. Drain and set aside. Toast the pine nuts over medium heat until golden brown. Remove from heat and set aside.
3. Combine the fresh basil leaves, grated Parmesan cheese, minced garlic, and extra-virgin olive oil in a food blender. Process until smooth. Combine the cooked farfalle pasta, boiled potatoes and green beans, and pesto sauce in a bowl. Toss well to coat all the ingredients.
4. Powder it with salt and crushed pepper to taste. Sprinkle the toasted pine over the pasta.
5. Serve the Farfalle with Pesto, Potatoes, and Green Beans warm or at room temperature.

Nutritions

Calories: 380 , Fat: 15g , Protein: 10g , Carbohydrate: 50g

PREPARATION TIME: 15 MIN

COOKING TIME: 15 MIN

SERVINGS: 4

LINGUINE WITH MUSSELS IN TOMATO SAUCE

Ingredients

- 8 ounces of linguine pasta
- 2 pounds fresh mussels, cleaned and debearded
- 2 tablespoons extra-virgin olive oil
- 4 cloves garlic, minced
- 1/4 teaspoon red pepper flakes
- 1 cup cherry tomatoes, halved
- 1/2 cup white wine
- 1/4 cup chopped fresh parsley
- Salt and black pepper to taste

Directions

1. Prepare linguine pasta as directed by package instructions until al dente. Drain and set aside. In a skillet, heat two tbsp oil over medium heat. Add minced garlic with red pepper flakes. Sauté for about 1-2 minutes until the garlic is fragrant.
2. Add cherry tomatoes and cook for 2-3 minutes until they soften. Add white wine and bring it to a simmer. Add cleaned mussels to the skillet, cover, and cook for about 5-7 minutes or until the mussels have opened.
3. Remove any unopened mussels from the skillet. Powder the sauce with salt and crushed pepper to taste.
4. Add prepared linguine to the skillet and toss it with the mussel and tomato sauce. Before serving, sprinkle chopped fresh parsley over the Linguine with Mussels in Tomato Sauce.

Nutritions

Calories: 400 , Fat: 8g , Protein: 25g , Carbohydrate: 55g

PREPARATION TIME: 15 MIN

COOKING TIME: 20 MIN

SERVINGS: 4

WHOLE GRAIN PENNE WITH BROCCOLI AND ANCHOVIES

Ingredients

- 8 ounces whole grain penne pasta
- 2 cups broccoli florets
- 2 tablespoons extra-virgin olive oil
- 4 anchovy fillets, minced
- 4 cloves garlic, minced
- 1/2 teaspoon red pepper flakes
- Juice of 1 lemon
- Grated Parmesan cheese (optional for serving)
- Salt and black pepper to taste

Directions

1. Prepare whole grain penne pasta as directed by package instructions until al dente. Drain and set aside.
2. Steam the broccoli florets for five minutes until they are tender-crisp. Set aside. In a non-stick skillet, heat two tbsp oil over medium heat.
3. Add minced anchovies, garlic, and red pepper flakes. Sauté for about 1-2 minutes until the garlic is fragrant and the anchovies have dissolved. Add prepared penne pasta and steamed broccoli to the skillet. Toss well to coat all the ingredients with the anchovy-garlic sauce.
4. Squeeze the lemon juice over the pasta and powder it with salt and crushed pepper to taste. Serve the Whole Grain Penne with Broccoli and Anchovies hot. Sprinkle with grated Parmesan cheese if desired.

Nutritions

Calories: 350 , Fat: 10g , Protein: 12g , Carbohydrate: 55g

PREPARATION TIME: 10 MIN

COOKING TIME: 15 MIN

SERVINGS: 4

MEDITERRANEAN PASTA WITH OLIVES, CAPERS, AND TUNA

Ingredients

- 8 ounces whole wheat spaghetti
- 2 tablespoons extra-virgin olive oil
- 2 cloves garlic, minced
- 1/4 teaspoon red pepper flakes
- 1 cup cherry tomatoes, halved
- 1/4 cup Kalamata olives, destoned and chopped
- 2 tablespoons capers
- 1 can (5 oz weight) tuna in water, drained and flaked
- 1/4 cup chopped fresh parsley
- Salt and black pepper to taste

Directions

1. Cook the whole wheat spaghetti according to the package instructions until al dente. Set aside
2. after draining.
3. Warm the two tbsp oil in a non-stick pan over medium heat. Combine the minced garlic and red pepper flakes in a mixing bowl. Cook for two minutes until the garlic is aromatic.
4. Cook the cherry tomatoes in the skillet for 2-3 minutes or until they soften. Combine the Kalamata olives, capers, and tuna flakes in a mixing bowl. Cook for three minutes to allow the ingredients to warm up.
5. Add spaghetti to the skillet and toss it with the olive, tomato, and tuna.
6. Stir in the chopped fresh parsley and season with salt and black pepper to taste.
7. Serve the Mediterranean Pasta with Olives, Capers, and Tuna hot.

Nutritions

Calories: 380 , Fat: 10g , Protein: 20g , Carbohydrate: 55g

PREPARATION TIME: 10 MIN

COOKING TIME: 15 MIN

SERVINGS: 4

SPAGHETTI WITH SEAFOOD MARINARA

Ingredients

- 8 ounces whole wheat spaghetti
- 2 tablespoons olive oil
- 4 cloves garlic, minced
- ½ teaspoon red pepper flakes
- 1 can (14 ounces) diced tomatoes
- ½ cup tomato sauce
- ½ cup dry white wine
- ½ cup vegetable broth
- ½ lb. mixed seafood (such as shrimp, mussels, and calamari)
- ¼ cup chopped fresh basil
- Salt and black pepper to taste

Directions

1. Prepared whole wheat spaghetti as directed by package instructions until al dente. Drain and set aside.
2. In a skillet, heat two tbsp oil over medium heat. Add minced garlic and red pepper flakes. Sauté for about 1-2 minutes until the garlic is fragrant.
3. Add diced tomatoes, tomato sauce, white wine, and vegetable broth to the skillet. Take this mixture to a simmer and let it sit for 10 minutes to let the flavors meld. Cook for 6-7 minutes until the seafood is cooked in the skillet with the mixed seafood.
4. Stir in the chopped fresh basil and season with salt and black pepper to taste. Serve the Spaghetti with Seafood Marinara hot.

Nutritions

Calories: 380 , Fat: 8g , Protein: 20g , Carbohydrate: 55g

PREPARATION TIME: 10 MIN

COOKING TIME: 20 MIN

SERVINGS: 4

WHOLE GRAIN PASTA WITH ROASTED RED PEPPER SAUCE

Ingredients

- 8 oz. whole grain penne pasta
- 2 large red bell peppers
- 2 tablespoons olive oil
- 2 cloves garlic, minced
- ¼ teaspoon red pepper flakes
- 1 can (14 ounces) diced tomatoes
- ¼ cup tomato paste
- ¼ cup vegetable broth
- 2 tablespoons chopped fresh basil
- Salt and black pepper to taste

Directions

1. Prepare the whole grain penne pasta as directed by package instructions until al dente. Drain and set aside. Set the oven heat to 450°F (230°C). Place the red bell peppers on the roasting sheet and roast for 20 minutes.
2. Remove the roasted bell peppers from the oven and transfer them to a bowl. Cover the bowl with a plastic sheet and let the peppers steam for 10 minutes. Peel the skins off the roasted bell peppers, remove the stems and seeds, and chop the flesh into small pieces.
3. In a non-stick skillet, heat two tbsp oil over medium heat. Add minced garlic with red pepper flakes. Sauté for about 1-2 minutes until the garlic is fragrant. Add diced tomatoes, tomato paste, vegetable broth, and roasted red peppers to the skillet.
4. Take this mixture to a simmer and continue cooking for 10 minutes to allow the flavors to meld together. Use the immersion/regular food blender to blend it until smooth. Return the sauce to the skillet and stir in the chopped fresh basil. Powder it with salt and black pepper to taste.
5. Add prepared penne pasta and toss it with the roasted red pepper sauce. Serve the Whole Grain Pasta with Roasted Red Pepper Sauce hot.

Nutritions

Calories: 380 , Fat: 8g , Protein: 12g , Carbohydrate: 68g

PREPARATION TIME: 15 MIN

COOKING TIME: 30 MIN

SERVINGS: 4

FUSILLI WITH MEDITERRANEAN VEGETABLE SAUTE

Ingredients

- 8 ounces whole wheat fusilli pasta
- 2 tablespoons olive oil
- 1 medium eggplant, diced
- 1 zucchini, diced
- 1 yellow bell pepper, diced
- 1 red onion, thinly sliced
- 3 cloves garlic, minced
- 1 teaspoon dried oregano
- 1/2 teaspoon dried basil
- 1/2 teaspoon dried thyme
- Salt and black pepper to taste
- Fresh parsley, chopped (for garnish)

Directions

1. aside. In a non-stick skillet, heat two tbsp oil over medium heat. Add diced eggplant, zucchini, bell pepper, and red onion. Sauté for about 5-7 minutes until the vegetables are tender.
2. Add minced garlic, dried oregano, dried basil, and dried thyme to the skillet. Powder it with salt, crushed black pepper to taste. Cook for 2-3 minutes. Add prepared fusilli pasta to the skillet and toss it with the sautéed vegetables.
3. Garnish with fresh parsley.
4. Serve the Fusilli with Mediterranean Vegetable Sauté hot.

Nutritions

Calories: 320 , Fat: 8g , Protein: 10g , Carbohydrate: 55g

PREPARATION TIME: 10 MIN

COOKING TIME: 15 MIN

SERVINGS: 4

PENNE WITH SHRIMP, FETA, AND TOMATOES

Ingredients

- 8 ounces whole wheat penne pasta
- 1 tablespoon olive oil
- 1 pound shrimp, peeled and deveined
- 4 cloves garlic, minced
- 1-pint cherry tomatoes, halved
- 1/2 cup crumbled feta cheese
- 2 tablespoons chopped fresh parsley
- Salt and black pepper to taste

Directions

1. Prepare whole wheat penne pasta as directed by package instructions until al dente. Drain and set aside.
2. In a non-stick skillet, heat two tbsp oil over medium heat. Add minced garlic and sauté for about 1 minute until fragrant.
3. Add shrimp and cook for 3-4 minutes. Add cherry tomatoes and cook for 2-3 minutes until they soften slightly. Stir in the cooked penne pasta and crumbled feta cheese. Toss well until all are well combined and the cheese starts to melt.
4. Powder it with salt and black pepper to taste. Garnish with chopped fresh parsley. Serve the Penne with Shrimp, Feta, and Tomatoes hot.

Nutritions

Calories: 380 , Fat: 9g , Protein: 30g , Carbohydrate: 44g

PREPARATION TIME: 15 MIN

COOKING TIME: 15 MIN

SERVINGS: 4

GREEK-STYLE LASAGNA (PASTITSIO)

Ingredients

- 12 oz. whole wheat lasagna noodles
- 1 lb. lean ground beef
- 1 medium onion, chopped
- 3 cloves garlic, minced
- 1 can (14 ounces) diced tomatoes
- ¼ cup tomato paste
- 1/2 cup red wine (optional)
- 1 teaspoon dried oregano
- 1/2 teaspoon cinnamon
- Salt and black pepper to taste
- 2 cups low-fat Greek yogurt
- 1/2 cup grated Parmesan cheese
- 1/2 cup breadcrumbs

Directions

1. Set the oven heat to 375°F (190°C). Prepare whole wheat lasagna noodles as directed by package instructions until al dente. Drain and set aside. In a non-stick skillet, cook the ground beef, chopped onion and garlic over medium heat until the beef is browned.
2. Drain any excess fat. Add diced tomatoes, tomato paste, red wine (if using), dried oregano, cinnamon, salt, and crushed pepper to the skillet. Stir to combine and simmer for 13-15 minutes. Mix the Greek yogurt, grated Parmesan cheese, salt, and black pepper in the other bowl.
3. Layer half of the cooked lasagna noodles in a greased baking dish. Spread half of the meat sauce over the noodles, followed by half of the yogurt mixture. Repeat the layers with the remaining noodles, meat sauce, and yogurt mixture.
4. Sprinkle breadcrumbs over the top layer. Bake for 33-35 minutes until golden and bubbly. Rest the lasagna to cool for a few minutes before slicing and serving.

Nutritions

Calories: 420 , Fat: 12g , Protein: 28g , Carbohydrate: 51g

PREPARATION TIME: 30 MIN

COOKING TIME: 60 MIN

SERVINGS: 8

Chapter 8:

20 Mediterranean Rice Recipes

BROWN RICE SALAD WITH FETA AND OLIVES

Ingredients

- 1 cup brown rice
- 2 cups water
- 1 cucumber, diced
- 1 red bell pepper, diced
- 1/4 cup diced red onion
- 1/2 cup pitted Kalamata olives, halved
- 1/2 cup crumbled feta cheese
- 2 tablespoons chopped fresh parsley
- 2 tablespoons lemon juice
- 2 tablespoons extra-virgin olive oil
- Salt and black pepper to taste

Directions

1. In a non-stick saucepan, add water to a boil. Add brown rice and decrease the stove heat to low. Cover and simmer for 37-40 minutes. Remove from heat and let it cool.
2. Combine the prepared brown rice with cucumber, red bell pepper, red onion, Kalamata olives, feta cheese, and chopped parsley in a bowl. Whisk the lemon juice, extra-virgin olive oil, salt, and black pepper in another small bowl.
3. Pour the lemon oil dressing over the rice salad and toss to coat. Serve the Mediterranean Brown Rice Salad chilled or at room temperature.

Nutritions

Calories: 280 , Fat: 12g , Protein: 7g , Carbohydrate: 37g

PREPARATION TIME: 15 MIN

COOKING TIME: 40 MIN

SERVINGS: 4

GREEK LEMON AND HERB BROWN RICE

Ingredients

- 1 cup brown rice
- 2 cups water
- 2 tablespoons fresh lemon juice
- 1 tablespoon extra-virgin olive oil
- 2 cloves garlic, minced
- 1 teaspoon dried oregano
- ½ teaspoon dried thyme
- Salt to taste

Directions

1. In a saucepan, add water and take a boil. Add brown rice, then decrease the stove heat to low. Cover and simmer for 37-40 minutes until the rice is tender. Remove from heat and rest it for 5 minutes.
2. Whisk the fresh lemon juice in a small bowl with extra-virgin olive oil, minced garlic, dried oregano, dried thyme, and salt. Fluff the prepared brown rice with a spatula/fork and pour the lemon and herb mixture over the rice.
3. Gently stir to combine and allow the flavors to blend for a few minutes. Serve the Greek Lemon and Herb Brown Rice as a side dish with your favorite Mediterranean meals.

Nutritions

Calories: 190 , Fat: 4g , Protein: 4g , Carbohydrate: 35g

PREPARATION TIME: 5 MIN

COOKING TIME: 40 MIN

SERVINGS: 4

BROWN RICE PAELLA WITH SEAFOOD

Ingredients

- 1 cup brown rice
- 2 cups vegetable broth
- 1 tablespoon olive oil
- 1 onion, diced
- 2 cloves garlic, minced
- 1 red bell pepper, diced
- 1 yellow bell pepper, diced
- 1 tomato, diced
- 1 teaspoon smoked paprika
- ½ teaspoon turmeric
- ½ teaspoon dried oregano
- ½ teaspoon dried thyme
- ½ teaspoon salt
- ¼ teaspoon black pepper
- ½ cup frozen peas
- 8 ounces mixed seafood (shrimp, mussels, calamari, etc.)
- Lemon wedges for serving
- Chopped fresh parsley for garnish

Directions

1. In a non-stick skillet, heat one tbsp of oil over medium heat. Add onion with garlic and sauté until they become translucent. Add red & yellow bell pepper. Cook for 5 minutes until the vegetables are slightly softened.
2. Stir in the smoked paprika, turmeric, oregano, thyme, salt, and black pepper. Cook for 1 minute to release the flavors. Add brown rice to the skillet and stir to coat it with the spices and vegetables.
3. Add vegetable broth and take this mixture to a boil. Decrease the stove heat to low, cover the skillet, and simmer for 37-40 minutes until the rice is tender.
4. Add frozen peas and mixed seafood. Cover the skillet and cook for 5 minutes until the seafood is done thoroughly. Remove from heat and rest it for a few minutes before serving.
5. Garnish with parsley and serve the Brown Rice Paella with Seafood with lemon wedges on the side.

Nutritions

Calories: 330 , Fat: 5g , Protein: 18g , Carbohydrate: 53g

PREPARATION TIME: 15 MIN

COOKING TIME: 40 MIN

SERVINGS: 4

MEDITERRANEAN VEGETABLE AND BROWN RICE STIR-FRY

Ingredients

- 1 cup brown rice
- 2 cups vegetable broth
- 2 tablespoons low-sodium soy sauce
- 1 tablespoon sesame oil
- 2 cloves garlic, minced
- 1 teaspoon grated fresh ginger
- 1 small onion, sliced
- 1 red bell pepper, sliced
- 1 yellow bell pepper, sliced
- 1 zucchini, sliced
- 1 cup sliced mushrooms
- 1 cup broccoli florets
- 1 cup snap peas
- 1 tablespoon sesame seeds (optional)
- Chopped green onions for garnish

Directions

1. In a saucepan, add vegetable broth to a boil. Add the brown rice and reduce the heat to low. Cover and simmer for 35-40 minutes.
2. In a bowl, whisk the low-sodium soy sauce with sesame oil. Set aside. Put the non-stick skillet over medium heat. Add minced garlic, grated ginger, and sauté for 1 minute until fragrant.
3. Add sliced onion, red bell pepper, yellow bell pepper, zucchini, mushrooms, broccoli florets, and snap peas to the skillet. Stir-fry for 5-7 minutes.
4. Push the vegetables to the other side of the skillet and add prepared brown rice to the other side. Pour the soy sauce and sesame oil mixture over the rice and stir-fry for 2 minutes to combine the flavors.
5. Sprinkle with sesame seeds (if using) and garnish with chopped green onions. Serve the Mediterranean Vegetable and Brown Rice Stir-fry as a main or side dish.

Nutritions

Calories: 280 , Fat: 6g , Protein: 7g , Carbohydrate: 51g

PREPARATION TIME: 10 MIN

COOKING TIME: 15 MIN

SERVINGS: 4

WILD RICE WITH ROASTED VEGETABLES AND TAHINI DRESSING

Ingredients

- 1 cup wild rice
- 2 cups vegetable broth
- 1 small eggplant, diced
- 1 red bell pepper, diced
- 1 zucchini, diced
- 1 yellow onion, sliced
- 2 tablespoons olive oil
- Salt and black pepper to taste
- 2 tablespoons tahini
- 2 tablespoons lemon juice
- 1 clove garlic, minced
- Water as needed

Directions

1. In a non-stick saucepan, add vegetable broth to a boil. Add wild rice and decrease the stove heat to low. Cover and simmer for 43-45 minutes until the rice is tender.
2. Set the oven heat to 400°F (200°C). Put diced eggplant with red bell pepper, zucchini, and sliced onion on the roasting sheet. Drizzle with oil and powder with salt and crushed pepper. Toss to coat the vegetables evenly.
3. Roast the vegetables for 23-25 minutes until golden and tender. Whisk the tahini, lemon juice, minced garlic, and water in a small bowl for a smooth dressing consistency.
4. In a bowl, combine the cooked wild rice and roasted vegetables. Drizzle the tahini dressing over the top and gently toss to coat everything. Serve the Wild Rice with Roasted Vegetables and Tahini Dressing as a nutritious and flavorful dish.

Nutritions

Calories: 290 , Fat: 11g , Protein: 8g , Carbohydrate: 43g

PREPARATION TIME: 15 MIN

COOKING TIME: 45 MIN

SERVINGS: 4

MEDITERRANEAN RICE SALAD WITH TUNA AND CAPERS

Ingredients

- 1 cup white or brown rice
- 2 cups water
- 1 can tuna, drained
- 1/4 cup chopped red onion
- 1/4 cup chopped Kalamata olives
- 2 tablespoons capers
- 1/4 cup chopped fresh parsley
- 2 tablespoons lemon juice
- 2 tablespoons extra-virgin olive oil
- Salt and black pepper to taste

Directions

1. In a saucepan, add water and take a boil. Add rice, then decrease the stove heat to low. Cover and simmer for 17-20 minutes. Remove from heat and let it cool.
2. In a bowl, flake the drained tuna with a spoon/fork. Add cooked rice with chopped red onion, Kalamata olives, capers, chopped parsley, lemon juice, extra-virgin olive oil, salt, and black pepper to the bowl with tuna.
3. Toss everything together until well combined. Adjust the seasoning if needed and refrigerate the salad for one hour (at least) to allow the flavors to meld.
4. Serve the Mediterranean Rice Salad with Tuna and Capers chilled as a satisfying and protein-rich meal.

Nutritions

Calories: 290 , Fat: 9g , Protein: 16g , Carbohydrate: 37g

PREPARATION TIME: 15 MIN

COOKING TIME: 20 MIN

SERVINGS: 4

BROWN RICE PILAF WITH PINE NUTS AND CURRANTS

Ingredients

- 1 cup brown rice
- 2 cups vegetable broth
- 1 tablespoon olive oil
- 1 small onion, chopped
- 1/4 cup pine nuts
- 1/4 cup currants
- 2 tablespoons chopped fresh parsley

Directions

1. In a non-stick saucepan, add vegetable broth and take a boil. Add brown rice and decrease the stove heat to low. Cover and simmer for 37-40 minutes.
2. In the other skillet, heat one tbsp oil over medium heat. Add chopped onion and sauté until it becomes translucent. Add pine nuts and toast them for a few minutes until they turn golden brown.
3. Stir in the cooked brown rice, currants, chopped fresh parsley, and salt. Mix everything until well combined. Remove from heat and rest it for a few minutes before serving.
4. Serve Brown Rice Pilaf with Pine Nuts and Currants as a delicious and nutritious side dish.

Nutritions

Calories: 230 , Fat: 8g , Protein: 5g , Carbohydrate: 36g

PREPARATION TIME: 10 MIN

COOKING TIME: 40 MIN

SERVINGS: 4

GREEK STUFFED TOMATOES WITH BROWN RICE (GEMISTA)

Ingredients

- 4 large tomatoes
- 1 cup cooked brown rice
- 1/2 cup chopped onion
- 1/2 cup chopped bell pepper
- 1/4 cup chopped fresh parsley
- 1/4 cup chopped fresh dill
- 2 tablespoons tomato paste
- 2 tablespoons olive oil
- 1/4 cup vegetable broth
- Salt and black pepper to taste

Directions

1. Set the oven heat to 375°F (190°C). Cut the tomatoes top to scoop out the flesh and seeds to create a hollow cavity. Reserve the tomato flesh for later use.
2. In a bowl, toss the cooked brown rice with chopped onion, chopped bell pepper, chopped fresh parsley, chopped fresh dill, tomato paste, olive oil, vegetable broth, salt, and black pepper. Mix everything until well combined.
3. Stuff each hollowed tomato with the rice mixture, pressing it down gently to fill the cavity. Put the stuffed tomatoes on the oven dish and pour the reserved tomato flesh and any leftover rice mixture around the tomatoes.
4. Cover the baking dish with foil paper and bake for 43-45 minutes until the tomatoes are tender and the rice is cooked. Remove from the oven and cool for a few minutes before serving. Serve the Greek Stuffed Tomatoes with Brown Rice (Gemista) as a delightful and satisfying Mediterranean meal.

Nutritions

Calories: 190 , Fat: 7g , Protein: 4g , Carbohydrate: 28g

PREPARATION TIME: 20 MIN

COOKING TIME: 50 MIN

SERVINGS: 4

WILD RICE SALAD WITH LEMON AND DILL

Ingredients

- 1 cup wild rice
- 2 cups vegetable broth
- 1/4 cup chopped red onion
- 1/4 cup chopped fresh dill
- 1/4 cup chopped fresh parsley
- Zest and juice of 1 lemon
- 2 tablespoons extra-virgin olive oil
- Salt and black pepper to taste

Directions

1. In a non-stick saucepan, add vegetable broth to a boil. Add wild rice, then decrease the stove heat to low. Cover and simmer for 37-40 minutes until the rice is tender. Remove from heat and let it cool.
2. In a bowl, toss the cooked wild rice with chopped red onion, chopped fresh dill, chopped fresh parsley, lemon zest, lemon juice, extra-virgin olive oil, salt, and crushed pepper. Mix everything until well combined.
3. Adjust the seasoning if needed, and refrigerate the salad for one hour to allow the flavors to meld. Serve the Wild Rice Salad with Lemon and Dill chilled as a refreshing and nutritious side dish.

Nutritions

Calories: 200 , Fat: 7g , Protein: 4g , Carbohydrate: 32g

PREPARATION TIME: 15 MIN

COOKING TIME: 40 MIN

SERVINGS: 4

BROWN RICE RISOTTO WITH MUSHROOMS AND SPINACH

Ingredients

- 1 cup brown rice
- 2 cups vegetable broth
- 1 tablespoon olive oil
- 1 small onion, chopped
- 2 cloves garlic, minced
- 8 ounces mushrooms, sliced
- 2 cups baby spinach
- 1/4 cup grated Parmesan cheese
- Salt and black pepper to taste

Directions

1. In a non-stick saucepan, add vegetable broth and take a boil. Add brown rice and decrease the stove heat to low. Cover and simmer for 37-40 minutes. Remove from heat and let it cool.
2. Heat one tbsp of oil over medium heat in the other non-stick skillet. Add chopped onion with smashed garlic, and sauté until they become translucent. Add sliced mushrooms and cook for three minutes.
3. Stir in prepared brown rice and baby spinach. Cook for two minutes until the spinach wilts. Remove from heat and add grated Parmesan cheese. Powder it with salt and crushed pepper to taste.
4. Serve the Brown Rice Risotto with Mushrooms and Spinach as a flavorful and satisfying meal.

Nutritions

Calories: 240 , Fat: 5g , Protein: 7g , Carbohydrate: 45g

PREPARATION TIME: 10 MIN

COOKING TIME: 40 MIN

SERVINGS: 4

WILD RICE WITH ROASTED EGGPLANT AND CHERRY TOMATOES

Ingredients

- 1 cup wild rice
- 2 cups vegetable broth
- 1 small eggplant, cubed
- 1 cup cherry tomatoes, halved
- 2 tablespoons olive oil
- 2 cloves garlic, minced
- 1 tablespoon chopped fresh basil
- Salt and black pepper to taste

Directions

1. Set the oven heat to 400°F (200°C). In a non-stick saucepan, add broth and take a boil. Add wild rice and decrease the stove heat to low. Cover and simmer for 37-40 minutes until the rice is tender.
2. Remove from heat and let it cool. Put the cubed eggplant and halved cherry tomatoes on a baking sheet. Drizzle the oil, then sprinkle minced garlic, chopped fresh basil, salt, and black pepper. Toss the coat evenly.
3. Roast for 27-30 minutes until the eggplant is tender. Toss the cooked wild rice, roasted eggplant, and cherry tomatoes in a bowl. Mix everything until well combined.
4. Adjust the seasoning if needed, and serve the Wild Rice with Roasted Eggplant and Cherry Tomatoes as a hearty and flavorful dish.

Nutritions

Calories: 220 , Fat: 8g , Protein: 6g , Carbohydrate: 32g

PREPARATION TIME: 15 MIN

COOKING TIME: 45 MIN

SERVINGS: 4

BROWN RICE SALAD WITH GRILLED VEGETABLES AND FETA

Ingredients

- 1 cup brown rice
- 2 cups vegetable broth
- 1 small zucchini, sliced lengthwise
- 1 red bell pepper, sliced
- 1 yellow bell pepper, sliced
- 1 red onion, sliced
- 2 tablespoons olive oil
- 2 tablespoons balsamic vinegar
- 1 tablespoon chopped fresh parsley
- 1/4 cup crumbled feta cheese
- Salt and black pepper to taste

Directions

1. In a non-stick saucepan, add broth and take a boil. Add brown rice, then decrease the stove heat to low. Cover and simmer for 37-40 minutes until the rice is tender. Remove from heat and let it cool.
2. Preheat a grill over medium-high heat. Brush the zucchini, bell peppers, and red onion slices with olive oil, then powder it with salt and black pepper. Grill the vegetables for 5-7 minutes per side until they are slightly charred and tender.
3. Remove from heat and put them aside to cool. Toss the prepared brown rice, grilled vegetables, balsamic vinegar, chopped fresh parsley, crumbled feta cheese, salt, and black pepper in a bowl. Toss everything together until well combined.
4. Adjust the seasoning if needed, and serve the Brown Rice Salad with Grilled Vegetables and Feta as a delicious and nutritious dish.

Nutritions

Calories: 240 , Fat: 8g , Protein: 6g , Carbohydrate: 37g

PREPARATION TIME: 20 MIN

COOKING TIME: 30 MIN

SERVINGS: 4

MEDITERRANEAN BROWN RICE AND SHRIMP STIR-FRY

Ingredients

- 1 cup brown rice
- 2 cups vegetable broth
- 1 pound shrimp, peeled and deveined
- 2 tablespoons soy sauce
- 2 tablespoons sesame oil
- 1 red bell pepper, sliced
- 1 yellow bell pepper, sliced
- 1 cup snow peas
- 1 carrot, sliced
- 2 cloves garlic, minced
- 1 tablespoon grated ginger
- 1 tablespoon chopped fresh cilantro
- Salt and black pepper to taste

Directions

1. In the non-stick stockpot, add vegetable broth and take a boil. Add brown rice, then decrease the stove heat to low. Cover and simmer for 37-40 minutes until the rice is tender. Remove from heat and let it cool.
2. In a bowl, marinate the shrimp in soy sauce for 10 minutes. Heat two tbsp oil in a non-stick skillet/wok over medium-high heat. Add marinated shrimp and cook for 2-3 minutes until they turn pink. Remove the shrimp and put it aside.
3. Add sliced bell peppers, snow peas, carrot, minced garlic, and grated ginger. Stir-fry for about 5 minutes until the vegetables are crisp-tender. Put the prepared shrimp back and add the cooked brown rice.
4. Stir everything and cook more for three minutes. Remove from heat, then top with fresh cilantro and powder with salt and crushed pepper to taste. Serve the Mediterranean Brown Rice and Shrimp Stir-fry as a flavorful and protein-packed meal.

Nutritions

Calories: 290 , Fat: 6g , Protein: 26g , Carbohydrate: 35g

PREPARATION TIME: 15 MIN

COOKING TIME: 15 MIN

SERVINGS: 4

LEMON AND HERB WILD RICE PILAF

Ingredients

- 1 cup wild rice
- 2 cups vegetable broth
- 1 tablespoon olive oil
- 1 small onion, chopped
- 2 cloves garlic, minced
- 1 tablespoon chopped fresh parsley
- 1 tablespoon chopped fresh dill
- Zest of 1 lemon
- Juice of 1 lemon
- Salt and black pepper to taste

Directions

1. In the stock pot, add vegetable broth and take a boil. Add wild rice, then decrease the stove heat to low. Cover and simmer for 37-40 minutes until the rice is tender. Remove from heat and let it cool.
2. Heat one tbsp oil in a non-stick skillet. Add chopped onion and minced garlic, and sauté until they become translucent. Stir in the cooked wild rice, chopped fresh parsley, chopped fresh dill, lemon zest, and lemon juice.
3. Cook for a few minutes until heated thoroughly. Powder with salt and black pepper to taste. Serve the Lemon and Herb Wild Rice Pilaf as a fragrant and refreshing side dish.

Nutritions

Calories: 180 , Fat: 3g , Protein: 5g , Carbohydrate: 36g

PREPARATION TIME: 10 MIN

COOKING TIME: 45 MIN

SERVINGS: 4

STUFFED ZUCCHINI WITH BROWN RICE AND GROUND LAMB

Ingredients

- 2 large zucchini
- ½ lb. ground lamb
- 1/2 cup cooked brown rice
- 1 small onion, chopped
- 2 cloves garlic, minced
- 1/4 cup chopped fresh parsley
- 1/4 cup chopped fresh mint
- 1/4 teaspoon ground cinnamon
- 1/4 teaspoon ground cumin
- Salt and black pepper to taste
- 1 cup tomato sauce

Directions

1. Set the oven heat to 375°F (190°C). Slice the zucchini to scoop out the flesh, leaving a hollow shell. Chop the zucchini flesh and set aside. In a non-stick skillet, cook the ground lamb over medium heat until browned.
2. Add chopped zucchini flesh with onion and minced garlic. Cook until the onion is soft. Stir in the cooked brown rice, chopped fresh parsley, chopped fresh mint, ground cinnamon, ground cumin, salt, and black pepper.
3. Cook for a few minutes until well combined. Spoon the filling into the hollowed-out zucchini shells. Place the stuffed zucchini in a baking dish. Pour the tomato sauce over the stuffed zucchini.
4. Cover the baking dish with foil paper and bake for 30 minutes. Remove the foil and bake for 10-15 minutes until the zucchini is tender. Serve the Stuffed Zucchini with Brown Rice and Ground Lamb as a satisfying and flavorful meal.

Nutritions

Calories: 260 , Fat: 14g , Protein: 17g , Carbohydrate: 18g

PREPARATION TIME: 20 MIN

COOKING TIME: 45 MIN

SERVINGS: 4

WILD RICE SALAD WITH ROASTED BUTTERNUT SQUASH

Ingredients

- 1 cup wild rice
- 2 cups vegetable broth
- 2 cups diced butternut squash
- 1 tablespoon olive oil
- 1/4 cup dried cranberries
- 1/4 cup chopped pecans
- 2 green onions, sliced
- 2 tablespoons chopped fresh parsley
- 2 tablespoons lemon juice
- Salt and black pepper to taste

Directions

1. In the non-stick stockpot, add vegetable broth and take a boil. Add wild rice, then decrease the stove heat to low. Cover and simmer for 37-40 minutes until the rice is tender. Remove from heat and let it cool.
2. Set the oven heat to 400°F (200°C). Put the diced butternut squash on the oven sheet and drizzle with olive oil. Toss the coat evenly. Roast in the preheated oven for 27-30 minutes until tender and slightly caramelized.
3. Combine the prepared wild rice with roasted butternut squash, dried cranberries, chopped pecans, sliced green onions, chopped fresh parsley, lemon juice, salt, and black pepper in a bowl. Toss to mix well.
4. Adjust the seasoning if needed. Serve Wild Rice Salad with Roasted Butternut Squash as a hearty and nutritious dish.

Nutritions

Calories: 280 , Fat: 9g , Protein: 5g , Carbohydrate: 48g

PREPARATION TIME: 15 MIN

COOKING TIME: 30 MIN

SERVINGS: 4

GREEK BROWN RICE WITH SPINACH AND FETA

Ingredients

- 1 cup brown rice
- 2 cups vegetable broth/water
- 1 tablespoon olive oil
- 1 small onion, diced
- 2 cloves garlic, minced
- 4 cups fresh spinach leaves
- ½ cup crumbled feta cheese
- 1 tablespoon lemon juice
- Salt and black pepper to taste

Directions

1. In a non-stick saucepan, add broth to a boil. Add brown rice, then decrease the stove heat to low. Cover and simmer for 37-40 minutes until the rice is tender. Remove from heat and let it cool.
2. Heat one tbsp oil in a non-stick skillet over medium heat. Add diced onion and minced garlic, and sauté until they become translucent. Add fresh spinach and cook until wilted.
3. Stir in the cooked brown rice, crumbled feta cheese, lemon juice, salt, and black pepper. Cook for a few minutes until heated thoroughly. Adjust the seasoning if needed.
4. Serve the Greek Brown Rice with Spinach and Feta as a flavorful and satisfying dish.

Nutritions

Calories: 220 , Fat: 7g , Protein: 7g , Carbohydrate: 32g

PREPARATION TIME: 10 MIN

COOKING TIME: 40 MIN

SERVINGS: 4

WILD RICE WITH POMEGRANATE AND PISTACHIOS

Ingredients

- 1 cup wild rice
- 2 cups vegetable broth
- ½ cup pomegranate arils
- ¼ cup chopped pistachios
- 2 tablespoons chopped fresh mint
- 1 tablespoon lemon juice
- 1 tablespoon olive oil
- Salt and black pepper to taste

Directions

1. In a saucepan, add vegetable broth and take a boil. Add wild rice, then decrease the stove heat to low. Cover and simmer for 37-40 minutes. Remove from heat and let it cool.
2. Toss the prepared rice, pomegranate arils, chopped pistachios, chopped fresh mint, lemon juice, olive oil, salt, and crushed pepper in a bowl. Toss to mix well.
3. Adjust the seasoning if needed. Serve with Pomegranate and Pistachios as a nutritious and flavorful side dish.

Nutritions

Calories: 230 , Fat: 9g , Protein: 6g , Carbohydrate: 34g

PREPARATION TIME: 10 MIN

COOKING TIME: 45 MIN

SERVINGS: 4

BROWN RICE AND LENTIL STUFFED CABBAGE ROLLS

Ingredients

- 12 cabbage leaves
- 1 cup cooked brown rice
- 1 cup cooked lentils
- 1 small onion, diced
- 2 cloves garlic, minced
- 1 carrot, grated
- 1/4 cup chopped fresh parsley
- 1 tablespoon olive oil
- 1 can (14 oz) crushed tomatoes
- 1 tablespoon tomato paste
- 1 teaspoon dried oregano
- Salt and black pepper to taste

Directions

1. Grab the large stockpot, add water, and boil it over medium heat. Add cabbage leaves and blanch them for 2-3 minutes. Drain and set aside. In a non-stick skillet, heat one tbsp of oil over medium heat.
2. Add diced onion and minced garlic, and sauté until they become translucent. Add grated carrot to the skillet and cook for two minutes until softened. Combine the cooked brown rice, lentils, sautéed onion mixture, chopped fresh parsley, dried oregano, salt, and black pepper in a bowl. Mix well.
3. Place 1/4 cup of the rice and lentil mixture onto each cabbage leaf. Roll tightly, tucking in the sides as you go. Mix the crushed tomatoes, tomato paste, and a pinch of salt and black pepper in the other bowl.
4. Spread a layer (thin) of the tomato mixture on the bottom of a baking dish. Place the stuffed cabbage rolls in the dish, seam side down. Pour the remaining tomato mixture over the rolls.
5. Cover the baking dish with foil paper and bake for 43-45 minutes. Remove the foil and bake for 15 minutes until the cabbage rolls are tender and the sauce is bubbly.
6. Serve the Brown Rice and Lentil Stuffed Cabbage Rolls as a comforting and nutritious meal.

Nutritions

Calories: 220 , Fat: 3g , Protein: 9g , Carbohydrate: 42g

PREPARATION TIME: 30 MIN

COOKING TIME: 60 MIN

SERVINGS: 6

MEDITERRANEAN BROWN RICE WITH GARLIC AND TOMATOES

Ingredients

- 1 cup brown rice
- 2 cups vegetable broth
- 2 tablespoons olive oil
- 3 cloves garlic, minced
- 1 small onion, diced
- 2 tomatoes, diced
- 1 tablespoon tomato paste
- 1 teaspoon dried oregano
- Salt and black pepper to taste
- Chopped fresh parsley for garnish

Directions

1. In a non-stick saucepan, add vegetable broth to a boil. Add brown rice and decrease the stove heat to low. Cover and simmer for 37-40 minutes until the rice is tender. Remove from heat and let it cool.
2. Heat two tbsp oil in a non-stick skillet over medium heat. Add minced garlic and diced onion, and sauté until they become translucent. Add diced tomatoes, tomato paste, dried oregano, salt, and black pepper to the skillet.
3. Cook for two minutes until the tomatoes soften and release their juices. Stir in the cooked brown rice and cook for 5 minutes.
4. Adjust the seasoning if needed. Top with chopped fresh parsley.

Nutritions

Calories: 220 , Fat: 7g , Protein: 5g , Carbohydrate: 37g

PREPARATION TIME: 10 MIN

COOKING TIME: 45 MIN

SERVINGS: 4

Chapter 9:

20 Mediterranean Salad Recipes

GREEK SALAD WITH FETA AND OLIVES

Ingredients

- 2 medium cucumbers, diced
- 4 medium tomatoes, diced
- 1 small red onion, thinly sliced
- 1 cup Kalamata olives, pitted
- 1 cup crumbled feta cheese
- 2 tablespoons extra-virgin olive oil
- 1 tablespoon red wine vinegar
- 1 teaspoon dried oregano
- Salt and black pepper to taste

Directions

1. Combine the cucumbers, tomatoes, red onion, olives, and feta cheese in a large bowl.
2. Mix the olive oil, red wine vinegar, dried oregano, salt, and pepper in a medium size mixing bowl.
3. Pour the dressing over the salad & mix it with a toss.
4. Serve the Greek Salad with Feta and Olives chilled.

Nutritions

Calories: 220 , Fat: 15g , Protein: 6g , Carbohydrate: 17g

PREPARATION TIME: 15 MIN

COOKING TIME: 0 MIN

SERVINGS: 4

QUINOA SALAD WITH LEMON VINAIGRETTE

Ingredients

- 1 cup cooked quinoa
- 1 cup diced cucumber
- 1 cup cherry tomatoes, halved
- 1/2 cup diced red bell pepper
- 1/4 cup chopped fresh parsley
- 2 tablespoons lemon juice
- 1 tablespoon extra-virgin olive oil
- 1 clove garlic, minced
- Salt and black pepper to taste

Directions

1. Mix cooked quinoa, cucumber, cherry tomatoes, red bell pepper, and parsley in a large bowl.
2. Mix lemon juice, olive oil, garlic, salt, and black pepper in a medium bowl.
3. Toss the dressing over the quinoa salad.
4. Refrigerate for 30 minutes before serving.

Nutritions

Calories: 180 , Fat: 6g , Protein: 6g , Carbohydrate: 27g

PREPARATION TIME: 20 MIN

COOKING TIME: 15 MIN

SERVINGS: 4

COUSCOUS SALAD WITH ROASTED VEGETABLES

Ingredients

- 1 cup couscous
- 1 cup diced zucchini
- 1 cup diced eggplant
- 1 cup cherry tomatoes
- 1/2 cup diced red onion
- 2 tablespoons extra-virgin olive oil
- 1 tablespoon lemon juice
- 1 teaspoon dried oregano
- Salt and black pepper to taste

Directions

1. Cook the couscous as directed on the package, then set it aside to cool.
2. Preheat the oven. Place diced zucchini, eggplant, cherry tomatoes, and red onion on a baking sheet. Drizzle olive oil, lemon juice, dried oregano, salt, and black pepper. Toss to coat.
3. Roast the vegetables for 20–25 minutes until tender.
4. In a big bowl, combine the prepared couscous and roasted vegetables. Mix well.
5. Serve the Couscous Salad with Roasted Vegetables at room temperature or chilled.

Nutritions

Calories: 220 , Fat: 8g , Protein: 5g , Carbohydrate: 34g

PREPARATION TIME: 15 MIN

COOKING TIME: 25 MIN

SERVINGS: 4

CHICKPEA SALAD WITH CUCUMBER AND TOMATOES

Ingredients

- 2 cups cooked chickpeas
- 1 cucumber, diced
- 1 cup cherry tomatoes, halved
- 1/4 cup chopped red onion
- 1/4 cup chopped fresh parsley
- 2 tablespoons lemon juice
- 2 tablespoons extra-virgin olive oil
- 1 teaspoon ground cumin
- Salt and black pepper to taste

Directions

1. Combine the cooked chickpeas, cucumber, cherry tomatoes, red onion, and parsley in a large bowl.
2. Whisk together the lemon juice, olive oil, ground cumin, salt & black pepper in a small bowl.
3. Mix everything thoroughly using a whisk after pouring the dressing over the chickpea salad.
4. Serve the Chickpea Salad with Cucumber and Tomatoes chilled.

Nutritions

Calories: 180 , Fat: 8g , Protein: 6g , Carbohydrate: 22g

PREPARATION TIME: 10 MIN

COOKING TIME: 0 MIN

SERVINGS: 4

MEDITERRANEAN TUNA SALAD WITH CAPERS

Ingredients

- 2 cans tuna, drained
- 1/2 cup diced red bell pepper
- 1/4 cup diced red onion
- 1/4 cup chopped Kalamata olives
- 2 tablespoons capers
- 2 tablespoons lemon juice
- 2 tablespoons extra-virgin olive oil
- 1 teaspoon Dijon mustard
- Salt and black pepper to taste

Directions

1. In a large bowl, flake the tuna with a fork.
2. Add the bell pepper, red onion, Kalamata olives, and capers to the bowl.
3. Whisk lemon juice, olive oil, Dijon mustard, salt, and pepper in a medium bowl.
4. Put the sauce over the tuna salad and throw it to mix.
5. Pour the sauce over the tuna salad and toss to mix.
6. Serve the Mediterranean Tuna Salad with chilled Capers.

Nutritions

Calories: 220 , Fat: 11g , Protein: 22g , Carbohydrate: 8g

PREPARATION TIME: 15 MIN

COOKING TIME: 0 MIN

SERVINGS: 4

GREEK FARRO SALAD WITH DILL AND FETA

Ingredients

- 1 cup cooked farro
- 1 cup diced cucumber
- 1 cup cherry tomatoes, halved
- 1/2 cup crumbled feta cheese
- 1/4 cup chopped fresh dill
- 2 tablespoons lemon juice
- 2 tablespoons extra-virgin olive oil
- Salt and black pepper to taste

Directions

1. Combine the cooked farro, cucumber, cherry tomatoes, feta cheese, and dill in a large bowl.
2. Mix lemon juice, olive oil, salt, and black pepper in a medium bowl.
3. Toss the dressing over the farro salad.
4. Serve the Greek Farro Salad with Dill and Feta chilled or at room temperature.

Nutritions

Calories: 240 , Fat: 9g , Protein: 9g , Carbohydrate: 32g

PREPARATION TIME: 15 MIN

COOKING TIME: 20 MIN

SERVINGS: 4

MEDITERRANEAN LENTIL SALAD WITH MINT

Ingredients

- 1 cup cooked lentils
- 1 cup diced cucumber
- 1 cup diced red bell pepper
- 1/2 cup chopped fresh mint leaves
- 1/4 cup crumbled feta cheese
- 2 tablespoons lemon juice
- 2 tablespoons extra-virgin olive oil
- Salt and black pepper to taste

Directions

1. Mix cooked lentils, cucumber, red bell pepper, mint, and feta cheese in a large bowl.
2. Mix lemon juice, olive oil, salt, and black pepper in a large bowl.
3. Pour dressing over lentil salad and mix.
4. Serve Mediterranean Lentil Salad with Mint cold or room temperature.

Nutritions

Calories: 240 , Fat: 10g , Protein: 12g , Carbohydrate: 28g

PREPARATION TIME: 15 MIN

COOKING TIME: 20 MIN

SERVINGS: 4

BULGUR SALAD (TABBOULEH)

Ingredients

- 1 cup cooked bulgur
- 1 cup diced cucumber
- 1 cup diced tomatoes
- 1/2 cup chopped fresh parsley
- 1/4 cup chopped fresh mint leaves
- 2 tablespoons lemon juice
- 2 tablespoons extra-virgin olive oil
- Salt and black pepper to taste

Directions

1. Mix the cooked bulgur, cucumber, tomatoes, parsley, and mint leaves in a big bowl.
2. Combine together the lemon juice, olive oil, salt, and black pepper in a small-sized bowl and stir well.
3. After pouring the sauce over the bulgur salad, toss it to combine the flavors.
4. The bulgur wheat used in tabbouleh gives this Mediterranean salad its distinctive texture. Either cold or at room temperature is OK for serving.

Nutritions

Calories: 200 , Fat: 7g , Protein: 6g , Carbohydrate: 30g

PREPARATION TIME: 15 MIN

COOKING TIME: 0 MIN

SERVINGS: 4

BEETROOT AND FETA SALAD

Ingredients

- 4 medium beetroots, cooked and diced
- 1/2 cup crumbled feta cheese
- 1/4 cup chopped fresh parsley
- 2 tablespoons lemon juice
- 2 tablespoons extra-virgin olive oil
- Salt and black pepper to taste

Directions

1. Bring together the diced beetroots, feta cheese, and parsley in a big bowl and mix well.
2. Mix lemon juice, olive oil, salt, and black pepper in a medium bowl.
3. After pouring the dressing over the beetroot salad, mix everything thoroughly.
4. Serve Mediterranean Beetroot and Feta Salad cold or at room temperature.

Nutritions

Calories: 180 , Fat: 10g , Protein: 6g , Carbohydrate: 18g

PREPARATION TIME: 15 MIN

COOKING TIME: 40 MIN

SERVINGS: 4

GREEK STYLE POTATO SALAD WITH OLIVES

Ingredients

- 4 medium potatoes, boiled and diced
- 1/2 cup sliced Kalamata olives
- 1/4 cup diced red onion
- 1/4 cup chopped fresh parsley
- 2 tablespoons lemon juice
- 2 tablespoons extra-virgin olive oil
- Salt and black pepper to taste

Directions

1. Dice potatoes, Kalamata olives, red onion, and parsley in a large bowl.
2. In a medium bowl, mix lemon juice, olive oil, salt, and black pepper.
3. Toss the potatoes with the dressing and stir to mix.
4. Serve Greek Style Potato Salad with Olives refrigerated or at room temperature.

Nutritions

Calories: 220 , Fat: 8g , Protein: 4g , Carbohydrate: 33g

PREPARATION TIME: 20 MIN

COOKING TIME: 20 MIN

SERVINGS: 4

GREEK-STYLE CABBAGE SLAW WITH LEMON AND FETA

Ingredients

- 4 cups shredded green cabbage
- 1/2 cup crumbled feta cheese
- 1/4 cup chopped fresh dill
- 2 tablespoons lemon juice
- 2 tablespoons extra-virgin olive oil
- Salt and black pepper to taste

Directions

1. Shred the cabbage, mix it with the feta cheese, and dill in a big small size bowl.
2. Combine lemon juice, olive oil, salt, and black pepper in a small basin.
3. Pour dressing over cabbage slaw and mix.
4. Serve Greek-style Cabbage Slaw with Lemon and Feta cold.

Nutritions

Calories: 120 , Fat: 9g , Protein: 4g , Carbohydrate: 8g

PREPARATION TIME: 15 MIN

COOKING TIME: 0 MIN

SERVINGS: 4

STUFFED AVOCADO SALAD

Ingredients

- 2 avocados
- 1 cup diced cucumber
- 1 cup diced tomatoes
- 1/2 cup crumbled feta cheese
- 2 tablespoons lemon juice
- 2 tablespoons extra-virgin olive oil
- Salt and black pepper to taste

Directions

1. Half the avocados and take out the pits.
2. Mix diced cucumber, tomatoes, and feta cheese in a medium bowl.
3. Combine lemon juice, olive oil, salt, and black pepper in a small basin.
4. Pour the dressing over the cucumber and tomato mixture and toss to combine.
5. Spoon the salad mixture into the avocado halves.
6. Serve the Mediterranean Stuffed Avocado Salad immediately.

Nutritions

Calories: 340 , Fat: 28g , Protein: 10g , Carbohydrate: 18g

PREPARATION TIME: 15 MIN

COOKING TIME: 0 MIN

SERVINGS: 2

EGGPLANT AND QUINOA SALAD

Ingredients

- 1 cup cooked quinoa
- 1 medium eggplant, diced
- 1 cup cherry tomatoes, halved
- 1/2 cup diced cucumber
- 1/4 cup chopped fresh parsley
- 2 tablespoons lemon juice
- 2 tablespoons extra-virgin olive oil
- Salt and black pepper to taste

Directions

1. Preheat the oven. Place the chopped eggplant on a sheet of parchment paper and drizzle with olive oil. Roast for 20 minutes until soft.
2. Mix cooked quinoa, roasted eggplant, cherry tomatoes, cucumber, and parsley in a large bowl.
3. In a medium bowl, mix lemon juice, olive oil, salt, and black pepper.
4. Put the dressing over the quinoa salad and mix it with your hands.
5. Serve the Mediterranean Eggplant and Quinoa Salad chilled or at room temperature.

Nutritions

Calories: 230 , Fat: 10g , Protein: 6g , Carbohydrate: 30g

PREPARATION TIME: 20 MIN

COOKING TIME: 20 MIN

SERVINGS: 4

WATERMELON AND FETA SALAD

Ingredients

- 4 cups cubed watermelon
- 1/2 cup crumbled feta cheese
- 1/4 cup sliced red onion
- 2 tablespoons chopped fresh mint leaves
- 2 tablespoons lemon juice
- 2 tablespoons extra-virgin olive oil
- Salt and black pepper to taste

Directions

1. Combine the cubed watermelon, feta cheese, red onion, and mint leaves in a large bowl.
2. Combine lemon juice, olive oil, salt, and black pepper in a small basin.
3. Pour the dressing over the watermelon salad and toss to combine.
4. Serve the Mediterranean Watermelon and Feta Salad chilled.

Nutritions

Calories: 110 , Fat: 6g , Protein: 3g , Carbohydrate: 13g

PREPARATION TIME: 10 MIN

COOKING TIME: 0 MIN

SERVINGS: 4

BARLEY SALAD WITH FRESH HERBS

Ingredients

- 1 cup cooked barley
- 1 cup diced cucumbers
- 1 cup cherry tomatoes, halved
- 1/4 cup chopped fresh parsley
- 2 tablespoons chopped fresh dill
- 2 tablespoons lemon juice
- 2 tablespoons extra-virgin olive oil
- Salt and black pepper to taste

Directions

1. Mix cooked barley, diced cucumbers, cherry tomatoes, parsley, and dill in a large bowl.
2. Mix lemon juice, olive oil, salt, and black pepper in a small bowl.
3. After pouring the dressing over the barley salad, mix everything thoroughly.
4. Serve Mediterranean Barley Salad with freshly chopped herbs cold or at room temperature.

Nutritions

Calories: 180 , Fat: 7g , Protein: 4g , Carbohydrate: 26g

PREPARATION TIME: 15 MIN

COOKING TIME: 45 MIN

SERVINGS: 4

GREEK-STYLE BROCCOLI SALAD WITH SUN-DRIED TOMATOES

Ingredients

- 4 cups chopped broccoli florets
- 1/4 cup sliced Kalamata olives
- 1/4 cup chopped sun-dried tomatoes
- 1/4 cup crumbled feta cheese
- 2 tablespoons lemon juice
- 2 tablespoons extra-virgin olive oil
- 1 clove garlic, minced
- Salt and black pepper to taste

Directions

1. Steam the chopped broccoli florets for 5 minutes or until crisp-tender. Rinse with cold water and drain.
2. Combine the steamed broccoli, Kalamata olives, sun-dried tomatoes, and feta cheese in a large bowl.
3. Mix lemon juice, olive oil, minced garlic, salt, and black pepper in a small bowl.
4. After pouring the dressing over the broccoli salad, mix everything thoroughly.
5. Chill Greek-style Broccoli Salad with Sun-Dried Tomatoes and serve.

Nutritions

Calories: 120 , Fat: 9g , Protein: 5g , Carbohydrate: 8g

PREPARATION TIME: 15 MIN

COOKING TIME: 5 MIN

SERVINGS: 4

KALE SALAD WITH KALAMATA OLIVES AND FETA

Ingredients

- 4 cups chopped kale leaves
- 1/4 cup sliced Kalamata olives
- 1/4 cup crumbled feta cheese
- 2 tablespoons lemon juice
- 2 tablespoons extra-virgin olive oil
- Salt and black pepper to taste

Directions

1. Mix chopped kale, Kalamata olives, and feta cheese in a sizable bowl.
2. In a medium bowl, mix lemon juice, olive oil, salt, and black pepper.
3. Pour the dressing that you made over the kale salad and toss to combine.
4. Leave the salad for a few minutes to soften the kale.
5. Serve cold Mediterranean Kale Salad with Kalamata Olives and Feta.

Nutritions

Calories: 130 , Fat: 10g , Protein: 5g , Carbohydrate: 7g

PREPARATION TIME: 10 MIN

COOKING TIME: 0 MIN

SERVINGS: 4

GREEK-STYLE CAULIFLOWER SALAD WITH LEMON AND OLIVES

Ingredients

- 4 cups cauliflower florets
- 1/4 cup sliced Kalamata olives
- 1/4 cup chopped fresh parsley
- 2 tablespoons lemon juice
- 2 tablespoons extra-virgin olive oil
- 1 clove garlic, minced
- Salt and black pepper to taste

Directions

1. Steam the florets of cauliflower for 5 minutes or until they are soft. Drain cold water.
2. Mix the steamed cauliflower, chopped Kalamata olives, and chopped parsley in a big bowl.
3. Mix lemon juice, olive oil, minced garlic, salt, and black pepper in a small bowl.
4. Put the dressing over the cauliflower a salad and toss to combine
5. Serve the Greek-style Cauliflower Salad with Lemon and Olives chilled.

Nutritions

Calories: 80 , Fat: 7g , Protein: 2g , Carbohydrate: 4g

PREPARATION TIME: 15 MIN

COOKING TIME: 5 MIN

SERVINGS: 4

MEDITERRANEAN ZUCCHINI AND WHITE BEAN SALAD

Ingredients

- 2 medium zucchini, spiralized or thinly sliced
- 1 can (15 oz) white beans, rinsed and drained
- 1/4 cup chopped fresh basil leaves
- 2 tablespoons lemon juice
- 2 tablespoons extra-virgin olive oil
- 1 clove garlic, minced
- Salt and black pepper to taste

Directions

1. Combine the spiralized or sliced zucchini, white beans, and chopped basil leaves in a large bowl.
2. Whisk together the chopped garlic, lemon juice, olive oil, salt, and black pepper in a bowl.
3. Pour the dressing over the zucchini and white bean salad and toss to combine.
4. Serve the Mediterranean Zucchini, and White Bean Salad chilled.

Nutritions

Calories: 160 , Fat: 7g , Protein: 7g , Carbohydrate: 18g

PREPARATION TIME: 10 MIN

COOKING TIME: 0 MIN

SERVINGS: 4

TOMATO AND CUCUMBER SALAD WITH RED ONION

Ingredients

- 2 large tomatoes, diced
- 1 English cucumber, diced
- 1/4 cup thinly sliced red onion
- 2 tablespoons chopped fresh parsley
- 2 tablespoons lemon juice
- 2 tablespoons extra-virgin olive oil
- Salt and black pepper to taste

Directions

1. Mix diced tomatoes, cucumber, sliced red onion, and chopped parsley in a bowl.
2. Mix lemon juice, olive oil, salt, and black pepper in a small bowl.
3. Put the dressing over the tomato and cucumber salad and mix to combine.
4. Chilled the Mediterranean Tomato and Cucumber Salad with Red Onion.

Nutritions

Calories: 80 , Fat: 5g , Protein: 2g , Carbohydrate: 8g

PREPARATION TIME: 10 MIN

COOKING TIME: 0 MIN

SERVINGS: 4

Chapter 10 :

20 Mediterranean Soup Recipes

GREEK LEMON CHICKEN SOUP (AVGOLEMONO)

Ingredients

- 4 cups chicken broth
- 2 cups cooked shredded chicken breast
- 1/2 cup cooked orzo pasta
- 3 eggs
- 1/4 cup lemon juice
- Salt and black pepper to taste
- Chopped fresh dill for garnish

Directions

1. In a pot, heat the chicken broth over medium heat.
2. Add shredded chicken and cooked orzo pasta to the pot and let simmer for 5 minutes.
3. Whisk the eggs with lemon juice in a bowl until well combined.
4. Slowly add the beaten egg mixture to the simmering soup, stirring continuously.
5. Continue to cook for five minutes, stirring occasionally.
6. Powder with salt and crushed black pepper to taste.
7. Serve the Greek Lemon Chicken Soup (Avgolemono) hot, garnished with chopped fresh dill.

Nutritions

Calories: 220 , Fat: 6g , Protein: 23g , Carbohydrate: 17g

PREPARATION TIME: 10 MIN

COOKING TIME: 30 MIN

SERVINGS: 4

MEDITERRANEAN LENTIL AND VEGETABLE SOUP

Ingredients

- 1 cup dried green lentils, rinsed
- 1 onion, diced
- 2 carrots, diced
- 2 celery stalks, diced
- 3 cloves garlic, minced
- 1 can (14 oz) diced tomatoes
- 4 cups vegetable broth
- 1 teaspoon dried oregano
- 1 teaspoon dried thyme
- Salt and black pepper to taste
- Chopped fresh parsley for garnish

Directions

1. In a large pot, combine the lentils, diced onion, carrots, celery, minced garlic, tomatoes, vegetable broth, dried oregano, and dried thyme.
2. Boil the mixture over medium heat, then decrease the stove heat and let simmer for 25-30 minutes.
3. Powder
4. with salt and crushed pepper to taste. Top with chopped fresh parsley.

Nutritions

Calories: 220 , Fat: 1g , Protein: 14g , Carbohydrate: 40g

PREPARATION TIME: 15 MIN

COOKING TIME: 30 MIN

SERVINGS: 6

TUSCAN BEAN SOUP WITH KALE AND PASTA

Ingredients

- 2 tablespoons olive oil
- 1 onion, diced
- 2 carrots, diced
- 2 celery stalks, diced
- 3 cloves garlic, minced
- 1 can (14 oz) cannellini beans, rinsed and drained
- 4 cups vegetable broth
- 1 cup small pasta
- 2 cups chopped kale leaves
- 1 teaspoon dried basil
- 1 teaspoon dried oregano
- Salt and black pepper to taste

Directions

1. In the deep-bottom pot, heat the olive oil over medium heat.
2. Add the diced onion, carrots, celery, and minced garlic to the pot. Sauté for 5 minutes or until the vegetables are tender.
3. Add the cannellini beans, vegetable broth, pasta, chopped kale leaves, dried basil, and dried oregano to the pot. Take a boil, then decrease the stove heat and simmer for 14-15 minutes until the pasta is cooked and the kale is wilted.
4. Powder with salt and crushed pepper to taste.
5. Serve the Tuscan Bean Soup with Kale and Pasta hot.

Nutritions

Calories: 230 , Fat: 4g , Protein: 9g , Carbohydrate: 41g

PREPARATION TIME: 10 MIN

COOKING TIME: 25 MIN

SERVINGS: 6

GREEK TOMATO SOUP WITH ORZO

Ingredients

- 2 tablespoons olive oil
- 1 onion, diced
- 2 cloves garlic, minced
- 1 can (14 oz) diced tomatoes
- 4 cups vegetable broth
- 1/2 cup orzo pasta
- 1 teaspoon dried oregano
- 1/2 teaspoon dried thyme
- Salt and black pepper to taste
- Chopped fresh parsley for garnish

Directions

1. Heat two tbsp oil over medium heat
2. in the large wok (with lid).
3. Add onion and minced garlic to the pot. Sauté for 5 minutes or until the onion is translucent.
4. Add the diced tomatoes (including the juice), vegetable broth, orzo pasta, dried oregano, and dried thyme to the pot. Bring to a boil, then decrease the burner heat and simmer for 17-20 minutes or until the orzo is cooked.
5. Powder the soup with salt and black pepper to taste.
6. Serve the Greek Tomato Soup with Orzo hot, garnished with chopped fresh parsley.

Nutritions

Calories: 180 , Fat: 4g , Protein: 5g , Carbohydrate: 32g

PREPARATION TIME: 10 MIN

COOKING TIME: 25 MIN

SERVINGS: 4

MEDITERRANEAN CHICKPEA AND RICE SOUP

Ingredients

- 1 tablespoon olive oil
- 1 onion, diced
- 2 carrots, diced
- 2 celery stalks, diced
- 3 cloves garlic, minced
- 1 can (14 oz) chickpeas, rinsed and drained
- 1/2 cup long-grain brown rice
- 4 cups vegetable broth
- 1 teaspoon ground cumin
- 1 teaspoon dried parsley
- Salt and black pepper to taste
- Chopped fresh cilantro for garnish

Directions

1. In the deep-bottom pot, heat the olive oil over medium heat.
2. Add the diced onion, carrots, celery, and minced garlic to the pot. Sauté for 5 minutes or until the vegetables are tender.
3. Add the chickpeas, brown rice, vegetable broth, ground cumin, and dried parsley to the pot. Bring to a boil, then decrease the burner heat and simmer for 23-25 minutes or until the rice is cooked and tender.
4. Powder the soup with salt and black pepper to taste.
5. Serve the Mediterranean Chickpea and Rice Soup hot, garnished with chopped fresh cilantro.

Nutritions

Calories: 220 , Fat: 4g , Protein: 9g , Carbohydrate: 39g

PREPARATION TIME: 10 MIN

COOKING TIME: 25 MIN

SERVINGS: 6

SPANISH-STYLE GAZPACHO

Ingredients

- 4 large tomatoes, diced
- 1 cucumber, peeled and diced
- 1 red bell pepper, seeded and diced
- 1 small red onion, diced
- 2 cloves garlic, minced
- 2 tablespoons extra-virgin olive oil
- 2 tablespoons red wine vinegar
- 1/2 teaspoon salt
- 1/4 teaspoon black pepper
- Chopped fresh basil for garnish

Directions

1. Combine the diced tomatoes, cucumber, red bell pepper, red onion, minced garlic, olive oil, red wine vinegar, salt, and black pepper in the high-power food blender. Blend until smooth.
2. Shift the mixture to a bowl and refrigerate for one hour (at least).
3. Serve the Spanish-style Gazpacho chilled, garnished with chopped fresh basil.

Nutritions

Calories: 100 , Fat: 7g, Protein: 2g , Carbohydrate: 9g

PREPARATION TIME: 15 MIN

COOKING TIME: 0 MIN

SERVINGS: 4

GREEK LENTIL SOUP (FAKES SOUPA)

Ingredients

- 1 cup dried brown lentils, rinsed
- 1 onion, diced
- 2 carrots, diced
- 2 celery stalks, diced
- 3 cloves garlic, minced
- 1 can (14 oz) diced tomatoes
- 4 cups vegetable broth
- 1 teaspoon dried oregano
- 1 teaspoon dried thyme
- Salt and black pepper to taste
- Chopped fresh parsley for garnish

Directions

1. In a large pot, combine the lentils, diced onion, carrots, celery, minced garlic, tomatoes, vegetable broth, dried oregano, and dried thyme.
2. Take this mixture to a boil over moderate heat, then minimize the heat and allow it to simmer for thirty to forty minutes or until the lentils have reached the desired tenderness.
3. Season to flavor with salt and black pepper.
4. Garnish the Greek Lentil Soup (Fakes Soupa) with minced fresh parsley and serve it hot.

Nutritions

Calories: 180 , Fat: 1g , Protein: 11g , Carbohydrate: 34g

PREPARATION TIME: 10 MIN

COOKING TIME: 40 MIN

SERVINGS: 6

VEGETABLE AND BARLEY SOUP

Ingredients

- 1 tablespoon olive oil
- 1 onion, diced
- 2 carrots, diced
- 2 celery stalks, diced
- 2 cloves garlic, minced
- 1 zucchini, diced
- 1 yellow squash, diced
- 1 red bell pepper, diced
- 1 can (14 oz) diced tomatoes
- 1/2 cup pearl barley
- 4 cups vegetable broth
- 1 teaspoon dried basil
- 1 teaspoon dried oregano
- Salt and black pepper to taste
- Chopped fresh parsley for garnish

Directions

1. Heat one tbsp oil over medium heat in the large wok (with lid).
2. Add the diced onion, carrots, celery, and minced garlic to the pot. Sauté for 5 minutes or until the vegetables are tender.
3. Add the diced zucchini, yellow squash, red bell pepper, diced tomatoes (including the juice), pearl barley, vegetable broth, dried basil, and dried oregano to the pot. Take a boil, then decrease the stove heat and let simmer for 30-40 minutes or until the barley is cooked and tender.
4. Powder with salt and crushed pepper to taste.
5. Serve the Mediterranean Vegetable and Barley Soup hot, garnished with chopped fresh parsley.

Nutritions

Calories: 170 , Fat: 2g , Protein: 5g , Carbohydrate: 34g

PREPARATION TIME: 15 MIN

COOKING TIME: 40 MIN

SERVINGS: 6

ITALIAN MINESTRONE SOUP

Ingredients

- 1 tablespoon olive oil
- 1 onion, diced
- 2 carrots, diced
- 2 celery stalks, diced
- 2 cloves garlic, minced
- 1 can (14 oz) diced tomatoes
- 4 cups vegetable broth
- 1 cup small pasta (such as macaroni or ditalini)
- 1 can (14 oz) cannellini beans, rinsed and drained
- 1 teaspoon dried basil
- 1 teaspoon dried oregano
- Salt and black pepper to taste
- Grated Parmesan cheese for garnish

Directions

1. In the deep-bottom pot, heat the olive oil over medium heat.
2. Add the diced onion, carrots, celery, and minced garlic to the pot. Sauté for 5 minutes or until the vegetables are tender.
3. Add the diced tomatoes (including the juice), vegetable broth, pasta, cannellini beans, dried basil, and dried oregano to the pot. Bring to a boil, then decrease the burner and simmer for 17-20 minutes or until the pasta is cooked.
4. Powder the soup with salt and black pepper to taste.
5. Serve the Italian Minestrone Soup hot, garnished with grated Parmesan cheese.

Nutritions

Calories: 220 , Fat: 4g , Protein: 10g , Carbohydrate: 38g

PREPARATION TIME: 15 MIN

COOKING TIME: 30 MIN

SERVINGS: 6

CHICKEN AND ORZO SOUP

Ingredients

- 2 chicken breasts, without skin and bone, cut into small pieces
- 1 tablespoon olive oil
- 1 onion, diced
- 2 carrots, diced
- 2 celery stalks, diced
- 3 cloves garlic, minced
- 4 cups chicken broth
- 1/2 cup orzo pasta
- 1 teaspoon dried thyme
- Salt and black pepper to taste
- Chopped fresh parsley for garnish

Directions

1. Warm the olive oil in a big pot over medium heat.
2. Cook the chicken in the saucepan until it is browned on all sides. Remove the chicken from the saucepan and set it aside.
3. Combine the diced onion, carrots, celery, and minced garlic in the same saucepan. Sauté the vegetables for four-five minutes or until tender.
4. Combine chicken with chicken broth, orzo pasta, dried thyme, salt, and black pepper in a saucepan. Decrease the burner heat to low and simmer for 18-20 minutes until the orzo and chicken are tender.
5. Serve the Mediterranean Chicken and Orzo Soup hot, garnished with chopped fresh parsley.

Nutritions

Calories: 260 , Fat: 5g , Protein: 28g , Carbohydrate: 23g

PREPARATION TIME: 10 MIN

COOKING TIME: 30 MIN

SERVINGS: 4

GREEK-STYLE MEATBALL SOUP (YOUVARLAKIA)

Ingredients

For the meatballs:

- 1 pound ground beef
- 1/2 cup breadcrumbs
- 1/4 cup grated onion
- 2 cloves garlic, minced
- 1/4 cup chopped fresh parsley
- 1/4 cup chopped fresh dill
- 1/4 cup grated Parmesan cheese
- 1 egg
- Salt and pepper to taste

For the soup:

- 1 onion, diced
- 2 carrots, diced
- 2 celery stalks, diced
- 3 cloves garlic, minced
- 4 cups vegetable broth
- 1 can (14 oz) diced tomatoes
- 1 teaspoon dried oregano
- Salt and pepper to taste
- Chopped fresh parsley for garnish

Directions

1. Combine all the meatball ingredients (ground beef, breadcrumbs, grated onion, minced garlic, chopped parsley, chopped dill, grated Parmesan cheese, egg, salt, and pepper). Stir until all of the ingredients are uniformly distributed.
2. Form the mixture into 1-inch diameter tiny meatballs.
3. In a large pot, heat some olive oil over medium heat. Add the diced onion, carrots, celery, and minced garlic. Sauté for 5 minutes or until the vegetables are tender.
4. Add the vegetable broth, diced tomatoes (including the juice), dried oregano, salt, and pepper to the pot. Bring to a boil.
5. Gently drop the meatballs into the boiling soup. Decrease the stove heat to low, cover, and simmer for 27-30 minutes or until the meatballs are cooked.
6. Serve the Greek-Style Meatball Soup (Youvarlakia) hot, garnished with chopped fresh

Nutritions

Calories: 280 , Fat: 12g , Protein: 22g , Carbohydrate: 20g

PREPARATION TIME: 20 MIN

COOKING TIME: 40 MIN

SERVINGS: 6

BUTTERNUT SQUASH AND QUINOA SOUP

Ingredients

- 1 butternut squash, peeled, seeded, and cubed
- 1 onion, diced
- 2 carrots, diced
- 2 celery stalks, diced
- 3 cloves garlic, minced
- 1/2 cup quinoa, rinsed
- 4 cups vegetable broth
- 1 teaspoon dried thyme
- Salt and pepper to taste
- Chopped fresh parsley for garnish

Directions

1. Combine the butternut squash, diced onion, carrots, celery, minced garlic, quinoa, vegetable broth, dried thyme, salt, and pepper
2. in a large pot.
3. Boil the mixture over moderate heat. Reduce the heat and let simmer for 20-25 minutes until the butternut squash and quinoa are cooked and tender.
4. Blend the soup until it turns in smooth and creamy.
5. Powder the soup with salt and crushed pepper if needed.
6. Serve the Mediterranean Butternut Squash and Quinoa Soup hot, garnished with chopped fresh parsley.

Nutritions

Calories: 160 , Fat: 1g , Protein: 5g , Carbohydrate: 36g

PREPARATION TIME: 15 MIN

COOKING TIME: 30 MIN

SERVINGS: 6

MEDITERRANEAN VEGETABLE AND LENTIL SOUP

Ingredients

- 1 tablespoon olive oil
- 1 onion, diced
- 2 carrots, diced
- 2 celery stalks, diced
- 3 cloves garlic, minced
- 1 zucchini, diced
- 1 yellow squash, diced
- 1 red bell pepper, diced
- 1 can (14 oz) diced tomatoes
- 1 cup dried green lentils, rinsed
- 4 cups vegetable broth
- 1 teaspoon dried oregano
- 1 teaspoon dried thyme
- Salt and pepper to taste
- Chopped fresh parsley for garnish

Directions

1. In the deep-bottom pan, heat one tbsp oil over medium heat.
2. Add the diced onion, carrots, celery, and minced garlic. Sauté for 5 minutes or until the vegetables are tender.
3. Add the diced zucchini, yellow squash, red bell pepper, tomatoes (including the juice), dried oregano, dried thyme, and rinsed lentils to the pot. Stir to combine.
4. Add vegetable broth and take a boil. Reduce the heat and let simmer for 30-40 minutes or until the lentils are tender.
5. Season with salt and pepper to taste.
6. Serve the Mediterranean Vegetable and Lentil Soup hot, garnished with chopped fresh parsley.

Nutritions

Calories: 210 , Fat: 2g , Protein: 11g , Carbohydrate: 38g

PREPARATION TIME: 10 MIN

COOKING TIME: 40 MIN

SERVINGS: 6

GREEK BEAN SOUP (FASOLADA)

Ingredients

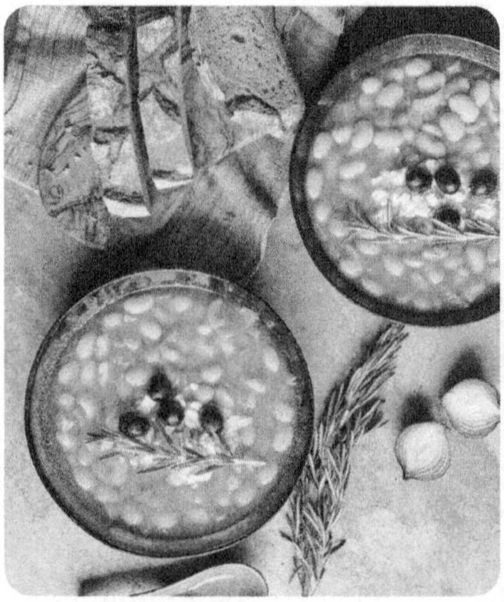

- 2 tablespoons olive oil
- 1 onion, diced
- 2 carrots, diced
- 2 celery stalks, diced
- 3 cloves garlic, minced
- 2 cups dried white beans, soaked
- 1 can (14 oz) diced tomatoes
- 6 cups vegetable broth
- 1 teaspoon dried oregano
- Salt and pepper to taste
- Chopped fresh parsley for garnish

Directions

1. In the deep-bottom pot, heat the olive oil over medium heat.
2. Add the diced onion, carrots, celery, and minced garlic. Sauté for 5 minutes or until the vegetables are tender.
3. Add the soaked and drained white beans, diced tomatoes (including the juice), vegetable broth, dried oregano, salt, and pepper to the pot. Take boil, then decrease the burner heat and simmer for 1 hour 30 minutes, or until the beans are cooked and tender.
4. Powder the soup with salt and pepper if needed.
5. Serve the hot Greek Bean Soup (Fasolada), garnished with chopped fresh parsley.

Nutritions

Calories: 260 , Fat: 4g , Protein: 14g , Carbohydrate: 47g

PREPARATION TIME: 10 MIN

COOKING TIME: 1 HR 30 MIN

SERVINGS: 6

ROASTED TOMATO AND RED PEPPER SOUP

Ingredients

- 4 large tomatoes, halved
- 2 red bell peppers, halved and seeded
- 1 onion, quartered
- 4 cloves garlic, peeled
- 2 tablespoons olive oil
- 4 cups vegetable broth
- 1 teaspoon dried basil
- 1 teaspoon dried oregano
- Salt and pepper to taste
- Chopped fresh basil for garnish

Directions

1. Set the oven heat to 400°F (200°C).
2. Place the halved tomatoes, red bell peppers, quartered onion, and peeled garlic cloves on a baking sheet. Drizzle with olive oil, then powder it with salt and pepper.
3. Roast the vegetables in the oven for 27-30 minutes.
4. Remove the vegetables from the oven and let them cool slightly. Then, peel the skin off the roasted red bell peppers.
5. Combine the roasted tomatoes, red bell peppers, roasted onion, garlic cloves, vegetable broth, dried basil, dried oregano, salt, and pepper in the food blender. Blend until smooth.
6. Transfer the mixture to a pot and heat over medium heat until warm. Top with fresh basil.

Nutritions

Calories: 140 , Fat: 7g , Protein: 3g , Carbohydrate: 19g

PREPARATION TIME: 15 MIN

COOKING TIME: 40 MIN

SERVINGS:

GREEK EGG AND LEMON SOUP WITH CHICKEN

Ingredients

- 4 cups chicken broth
- 2 cups cooked shredded chicken breast
- 1/2 cup orzo pasta
- 3 eggs
- 1/4 cup lemon juice
- Salt and pepper to taste
- Chopped fresh dill for garnish

Directions

1. In a pot, heat the chicken broth over medium heat.
2. Add shredded chicken and cooked orzo pasta to the pot. Let simmer for 5 minutes.
3. Whisk the eggs with lemon juice in a bowl until well combined.
4. Add egg mixture to the simmering soup, stirring continuously.
5. Continue to cook for five minutes, stirring occasionally.
6. Season with salt and pepper to taste. Top fresh dill.

Nutritions

Calories: 220 , Fat: 6g , Protein: 23g , Carbohydrate: 17g

PREPARATION TIME: 10 MIN

COOKING TIME: 1255 MIN

SERVINGS: 4

SPINACH AND WHITE BEAN SOUP

Ingredients

- 1 tablespoon olive oil
- 1 onion, diced
- 2 cloves garlic, minced
- 4 cups vegetable broth
- 2 cups packed fresh spinach leaves
- 1 can (14 oz) white beans, rinsed and drained
- 1 teaspoon dried oregano
- Salt and pepper to taste
- Grated Parmesan cheese for garnish

Directions

1. In a stockpot, heat one tbsp of oil over medium heat.
2. Add onion and minced garlic to the stockpot. Sauté for 5 minutes or until the onion is translucent.
3. Add the pot's vegetable broth, fresh spinach leaves, white beans, dried oregano, salt, and pepper. Take a boil, decrease the stove heat, and let simmer for 15 minutes.
4. Use your regular blender to blend the soup until smooth.
5. Sprinkle with salt and pepper if needed.
6. Serve the Mediterranean Spinach and White Bean Soup hot, garnished with grated Parmesan cheese.

Nutritions

Calories: 150 , Fat: 4g , Protein: 9g , Carbohydrate: 21g

PREPARATION TIME: 10 MIN

COOKING TIME: 25 MIN

SERVINGS: 4

GREEK-STYLE ZUCCHINI AND FETA SOUP

Ingredients

- 2 tablespoons olive oil
- 1 onion, diced
- 2 cloves garlic, minced
- 2 zucchini, diced
- 4 cups vegetable broth
- 1 teaspoon dried oregano
- Salt and pepper to taste
- Crumbled feta cheese for garnish
- Chopped fresh dill for garnish

Directions

1. In a stockpot, heat two tbsp olive oil over medium heat.
2. Add onion and minced garlic to the stockpot. Sauté for 5 minutes or until the onion is translucent.
3. Add the diced zucchini, vegetable broth, dried oregano, salt, and pepper to the pot. Bring to a boil, then decrease teh burner heat and simmer for 17-20 minutes or until the zucchini is tender.
4. Use the regular blender to blend the soup until smooth.
5. Powder the soup with salt and pepper if needed.
6. Serve the hot Greek-Style Zucchini and Feta Soup, garnished with crumbled feta cheese and chopped fresh dill.

Nutritions

Calories: 160 , Fat: 9g , Protein: 4g , Carbohydrate: 16g

PREPARATION TIME: 10 MIN

COOKING TIME: 25 MIN

SERVINGS: 4

SHRIMP AND ORZO SOUP

Ingredients

- 1 tablespoon olive oil
- 1 onion, diced
- 2 cloves garlic, minced
- 1 red bell pepper, diced
- 1 can (14 oz) diced tomatoes
- 4 cups vegetable broth
- 1/2 cup orzo pasta
- 1/2 teaspoon dried oregano
- 1/2 teaspoon dried basil
- 1/2 teaspoon dried thyme
- Salt and pepper to taste
- Cooked shrimp for garnish
- Chopped fresh parsley for garnish

Directions

1. In a non-stick stockpot, heat one tbsp of oil over medium heat.
2. Add the diced onion, minced garlic, and red bell pepper to the pot. Sauté for 5 minutes or until the vegetables are tender.
3. Add the diced tomatoes (including the juice), vegetable broth, orzo pasta, dried oregano, dried basil, dried thyme, salt, and crushed pepper to the pot. Take a boil, then decrease the burner heat and simmer for 19-20 minutes or until the orzo is cooked.
4. Powder the soup with salt and crushed pepper if needed.
5. Serve the Mediterranean Shrimp and Orzo Soup hot, garnished with cooked shrimp and chopped fresh parsley.

Nutritions

Calories: 210 , Fat: 4g , Protein: 10g , Carbohydrate: 35g

PREPARATION TIME: 10 MIN

COOKING TIME: 25 MIN

SERVINGS: 4

POTATO AND CHORIZO SOUP

Ingredients

- 1 tablespoon olive oil
- 1 onion, diced
- 2 cloves garlic, minced
- 2 potatoes, peeled and diced
- 4 cups vegetable broth
- 1/2 cup diced chorizo sausage
- 1 teaspoon dried thyme
- Salt and pepper to taste
- Chopped fresh parsley for garnish

Directions

1. In a stockpot, heat one tbsp of oil over medium heat.
2. Add onion and minced garlic to the stockpot. Sauté for 5 minutes or until the onion is translucent.
3. Add the diced potatoes, vegetable broth, chorizo sausage, dried thyme, salt, and crushed pepper to the pot. Take a boil, then decrease the stove heat and let simmer for 23-25 minutes or until the potatoes are tender.
4. Powder salt and crushed pepper if needed.
5. Serve the Mediterranean Potato and Chorizo Soup hot, garnished with chopped fresh parsley.

Nutritions

Calories: 240 , Fat: 10g , Protein: 7g , Carbohydrate: 32g

PREPARATION TIME: 10 MIN

COOKING TIME: 30 MIN

SERVINGS: 4

Chapter 11:

20 Mediterranean Balancing with Fruits Recipes

GREEK YOGURT WITH HONEY AND FRESH BERRIES

Ingredients

- 1 cup Greek yogurt
- 1 tablespoon honey
- 1/2 cup fresh mixed berries (such as strawberries, blueberries, and ra

Directions

1. In a bowl, add the Greek yogurt.
2. Drizzle the honey over the yogurt.
3. Top with fresh mixed berries.
4. Stir gently to combine.
5. Serve the Greek Yogurt with Honey and Fresh Berries immediately.

Nutritions

Calories: 200 , Fat: 0g , Protein: 20g , Carbohydrate: 30g

PREPARATION TIME: 5 MIN

COOKING TIME: 0 MIN

SERVINGS: 1

MEDITERRANEAN FIG AND GOAT CHEESE SALAD

Ingredients

- 4 cups mixed salad greens
- 4 fresh figs, sliced
- 2 ounces goat cheese, crumbled
- 2 tablespoons balsamic vinegar
- 1 tablespoon extra-virgin olive oil
- Salt and pepper to taste

Directions

1. Combine the mixed salad greens, sliced figs, and crumbled goat cheese in a salad bowl.
2. Whisk the balsamic vinegar with olive oil, salt, and pepper in a small bowl.
3. Drizzle the vinegar oil dressing over the salad and toss to coat.
4. Serve the Mediterranean Fig and Goat Cheese Salad immediately.

Nutritions

Calories: 180Fat: 11g , Protein: 6g , Carbohydrate: 18g

PREPARATION TIME: 10 MIN

COOKING TIME: 0 MIN

SERVINGS: 2

GREEK-STYLE BAKED APPLES WITH HONEY AND WALNUTS

Ingredients

- 4 apples (Granny Smith or Honeycrisp)
- 2 tablespoons honey
- 1/4 cup chopped walnuts
- 1 teaspoon ground cinnamon
- Greek yogurt for serving

Directions

1. Set the oven heat to 375°F (190°C).
2. Core the apples and cut a thin slice off the bottom of each apple so that they sit flat.
3. Place the apples in a baking dish.
4. Drizzle the honey over the apples.
5. In a small bowl, mix the chopped walnuts and ground cinnamon.
6. Stuff the mixture into the cavity of each apple.
7. Bake for 27-30 minutes until the apples are tender.
8. Serve the Greek-Style Baked Apples warm with a dollop of Greek yogurt.

Nutritions

Calories: 180 , Fat: 5g , Protein: 3g , Carbohydrate: 36g

PREPARATION TIME: 10 MIN

COOKING TIME: 30 MIN

SERVINGS: 4

MEDITERRANEAN CITRUS AND OLIVE SALAD

Ingredients

- 2 oranges, peeled and segmented
- 1 grapefruit, peeled and segmented
- 1/4 cup pitted Kalamata olives
- 2 tablespoons extra-virgin olive oil
- 1 tablespoon lemon juice
- Salt and pepper to taste
- Fresh mint leaves for garnish

Directions

1. Combine the orange, grapefruit, and Kalamata olives
2. in a bowl.
3. Whisk the extra-virgin olive oil with lemon juice, salt, and pepper in a small bowl.
4. Drizzle the dressing over the citrus and olive mixture and toss gently to combine.
5. Garnish with fresh mint leaves.
6. Serve the Mediterranean Citrus and Olive Salad immediately.

Nutritions

Calories: 160 , Fat: 13g , Protein: 2g , Carbohydrate: 11g

PREPARATION TIME: 10 MIN

COOKING TIME: 0 MIN

SERVINGS: 2

GRILLED PEACH AND MOZZARELLA SALAD

Ingredients

- 2 peaches, halved and pitted
- 4 cups arugula
- 4 ounces fresh mozzarella cheese, sliced
- 2 tablespoons balsamic vinegar
- 1 tablespoon extra-virgin olive oil
- Salt and pepper to taste

Directions

1. Over medium heat, preheat a grill or grill pan.
2. Cut side down, and place the peach halves on the grill for 3 to 4 minutes or until grill marks emerge.
3. The peaches should be taken from the grill and given time to cool.
4. Fresh mozzarella cheese and rocket should be combined in a salad bowl.
5. The peaches should be sliced and added to the salad.
6. Combine the balsamic vinegar, olive oil, salt, and pepper in a small bowl.
7. Toss the salad with the vinegar oil dressing after drizzling it over it.
8. Serve the Grilled Peach and Mozzarella Salad immediately.

Nutritions

Calories: 210 , Fat: 14g , Protein: 12g , Carbohydrate: 15g

PREPARATION TIME: 10 MIN

COOKING TIME: 4 MIN

SERVINGS: 2

MEDITERRANEAN PEAR AND ARUGULA SALAD WITH FETA

Ingredients

- 4 cups arugula
- 2 ripe pears, sliced
- 1/4 cup crumbled feta cheese
- 2 tablespoons balsamic vinegar
- 1 tablespoon extra-virgin olive oil
- Salt and pepper to taste
- Chopped walnuts for garnish

Directions

1. Combine the arugula, sliced pears, and crumbled feta cheese in a salad bowl.
2. Whisk the balsamic vinegar with olive oil, salt, and crushed pepper in a small bowl.
3. Drizzle the vinegar oil dressing over the salad and toss gently to coat.
4. Garnish with chopped walnuts.
5. Serve the Mediterranean Pear and Arugula Salad immediately.

Nutritions

Calories: 180 , Fat: 10g , Protein: 5g , Carbohydrate: 22g

PREPARATION TIME: 10 MIN

COOKING TIME:0 MIN

SERVINGS: 2

GREEK YOGURT PARFAIT WITH FRESH FRUITS AND HONEY

Ingredients

- 1 cup Greek yogurt
- 1/2 cup mixed fresh fruits (such as berries, sliced banana, and diced
- 1 tablespoon honey or maple syrup
- 2 tablespoons granola

Directions

1. Layerl, layer the Greek yogurt, then mix fresh fruits, honey, and granola in a glass or bowl.
2. Repeat the layers until all the elements are used.
3. Serve the Greek Yogurt Parfait with Fresh Fruits and Honey immediately.

Nutritions

Calories: 240 , Fat: 4g , Protein: 20g , Carbohydrate: 36g

PREPARATION TIME: 5 MIN

COOKING TIME: 0 MIN

SERVINGS: 2

MEDITERRANEAN AVOCADO AND STRAWBERRY SALAD

Ingredients

- 4 cups mixed salad greens
- 1 ripe avocado, sliced
- 1 cup sliced strawberries
- 2 tablespoons balsamic vinegar
- 1 tablespoon extra-virgin olive oil
- Salt and pepper to taste
- Chopped almonds for garnish

Directions

1. Combine the mixed salad greens, sliced avocado, and sliced strawberries in a salad bowl.
2. Whisk the balsamic vinegar with olive oil, salt, and crushed pepper in a bowl.
3. Drizzle the vinegar oil dressing over the salad and toss gently to coat.
4. Garnish with chopped almonds.
5. Serve the Mediterranean Avocado and Strawberry Salad immediately.

Nutritions

Calories: 200 , Fat: 14g , Protein: 4g , Carbohydrate: 18g

PREPARATION TIME: 10 MIN

COOKING TIME: 0 MIN

SERVINGS: 2

MEDITERRANEAN CITRUS AND FENNEL SALAD

Ingredients

- 2 oranges, peeled and sliced
- 1 grapefruit, peeled and sliced
- 1 small fennel bulb, thinly sliced
- 2 tablespoons lemon juice
- 1 tablespoon extra-virgin olive oil
- Salt and pepper to taste
- Fresh mint leaves for garnish

Directions

1. Combine the orange, grapefruit, and sliced fennel in a salad bowl.
2. Whisk the lemon juice with olive oil, salt, and crushed pepper in a small bowl.
3. Drizzle the lemon oil dressing over the salad and toss gently to coat.
4. Garnish with fresh mint leaves.
5. Serve the Mediterranean Citrus and Fennel Salad immediately.

Nutritions

Calories: 140 , Fat: 4g , Protein: 2g , Carbohydrate: 27g

PREPARATION TIME: 10 MIN

COOKING TIME: 0 MIN

SERVINGS: 2

MEDITERRANEAN APPLE AND CABBAGE SLAW

Ingredients

- 2 cups shredded green cabbage
- 1 large apple, julienned
- 1/4 cup chopped walnuts
- 2 tablespoons apple cider vinegar
- 1 tablespoon extra-virgin olive oil
- 1 teaspoon Dijon mustard
- Salt and pepper to taste

Directions

1. Combine the shredded green cabbage, julienned apple, and chopped walnuts in a large bowl.
2. Whisk the apple cider vinegar with olive oil, Dijon mustard, salt, and crushed pepper in a small bowl.
3. Drizzle the dressing over the cabbage mixture and toss to coat.
4. Serve the Mediterranean Apple and Cabbage Slaw immediately.

Nutritions

Calories: 120 , Fat: 8g , Protein: 2g , Carbohydrate: 12g

PREPARATION TIME: 10 MIN

COOKING TIME: 0 MIN

SERVINGS: 4

GREEK-STYLE CHERRY TOMATO AND WATERMELON SALAD

Ingredients

- 2 cups cherry tomatoes, halved
- 2 cups diced watermelon
- 1/4 cup crumbled feta cheese
- 2 tablespoons balsamic vinegar
- 1 tablespoon extra-virgin olive oil
- Salt and pepper to taste
- Fresh basil leaves for garnish

Directions

1. Combine the cherry tomato halves, diced watermelon, and crumbled feta cheese in a salad bowl.
2. Whisk the balsamic vinegar with olive oil, salt, and crushed pepper in a small bowl.
3. Drizzle the vinegar oil dressing over the salad and toss gently to coat.
4. Garnish with fresh basil leaves.
5. Serve the Greek-Style Cherry Tomato and Watermelon Salad immediately.

Nutritions

Calories: 120 , Fat: 6g , Protein: 4g , Carbohydrate: 15g

PREPARATION TIME: 10 MIN

COOKING TIME: 0 MIN

SERVINGS: 2

MEDITERRANEAN FRUIT SALAD WITH LEMON MINT DRESSING

Ingredients

- 2 cups mixed fresh fruits (such as melon, grapes, kiwi, and berries)
- 1 tablespoon lemon juice
- 1 tablespoon honey
- 1 tablespoon chopped fresh mint leaves

Directions

1. In a bowl, combine the mixed fresh fruits.
2. Whisk the lemon juice with honey and chopped fresh mint leaves in a small bowl.
3. Drizzle lemon honey e dressing over the fruit salad and toss gently to coat.
4. Serve the Mediterranean Fruit Salad with Lemon Mint Dressing immediately.

Nutritions

Calories: 80 , Fat: 0g , Protein: 1g , Carbohydrate: 20g

PREPARATION TIME: 15 MIN

COOKING TIME: 0 MIN

SERVINGS: 4

GREEK YOGURT WITH POMEGRANATE AND HONEY

Ingredients

- 1 cup Greek yogurt
- 1/2 cup pomegranate seeds
- 1 tablespoon honey

Directions

1. In a bowl, place the Greek yogurt.
2. Top with pomegranate seeds.
3. Drizzle with honey.
4. Serve the Greek Yogurt with Pomegranate and Honey immediately.

Nutritions

Calories: 200 , Fat: 0g , Protein: 20g , Carbohydrate: 30g

PREPARATION TIME: 5 MIN

COOKING TIME: 0 MIN

SERVINGS: 1

MEDITERRANEAN GRILLED PINEAPPLE WITH MINT AND HONEY

Ingredients

- 1 pineapple, peeled and cut into slices
- 2 tablespoons honey
- 2 tablespoons chopped fresh mint leaves
- Greek yogurt for serving

Directions

1. Preheat a grill over medium heat.
2. Grill the pineapple slices for 2-3 minutes for each side or until grill marks appear.
3. Remove the pineapple and cool it slightly.
4. In a bowl, whisk the honey with chopped fresh mint leaves.
5. Drizzle the honey and mint mixture over the grilled pineapple slices.
6. Serve the Mediterranean Grilled Pineapple with Mint and Honey with Greek yogurt

Nutritions

Calories: 160 , Fat: 0g , Protein: 1g , Carbohydrate: 40g

PREPARATION TIME: 10 MIN

COOKING TIME: 5 MIN

SERVINGS: 2

MEDITERRANEAN MANGO AND AVOCADO SALAD

Ingredients

- 2 cups mixed salad greens
- 1 ripe mango, peeled and diced
- 1 ripe avocado, peeled and diced
- 2 tablespoons lime juice
- 1 tablespoon extra-virgin olive oil
- Salt and pepper to taste
- Chopped fresh cilantro for garnish

Directions

1. Combine the mixed salad greens, diced mango, and avocado in a salad bowl.
2. Beat the lime juice with olive oil, salt, and crushed pepper in a bowl.
3. Drizzle the lemon oil dressing over the salad and toss gently to coat.
4. Garnish with chopped fresh cilantro.
5. Serve the Mediterranean Mango and Avocado Salad immediately.

Nutritions

Calories: 200 , Fat: 15g, Protein: 2g , Carbohydrate: 18g

PREPARATION TIME: 10 MIN

COOKING TIME: 0 MIN

SERVINGS: 2

GREEK-STYLE BAKED PEARS WITH WALNUTS AND HONEY

Ingredients

- 2 ripe pears, halved and cored
- 2 tablespoons chopped walnuts
- 2 tablespoons honey
- 1/2 teaspoon ground cinnamon
- Greek yogurt for serving

Directions

1. Set the oven heat to 375°F (190°C).
2. Place the pear halves, cut side up, in a baking dish.
3. Combine the chopped walnuts, honey, and ground cinnamon in a small bowl.
4. Spoon the walnut mixture into the center of each pear half.
5. Bake for 20 minutes or until the pears are tender and slightly caramelized.
6. Serve the Greek-Style Baked Pears warm with a side of Greek yogurt.

Nutritions

Calories: 180 , Fat: 6g , Protein: 2g, Carbohydrate: 36g

PREPARATION TIME: 10 MIN

COOKING TIME: 20 MIN

SERVINGS: 2

MEDITERRANEAN MELON AND PROSCIUTTO SALAD

Ingredients

- 2 cups diced melon (such as cantaloupe or honeydew)
- 4 slices prosciutto, torn into pieces
- 2 cups arugula
- 1 tablespoon balsamic vinegar
- 1 tablespoon extra-virgin olive oil
- Salt and pepper to taste

Directions

1. Combine the diced melon, torn prosciutto, and arugula in a salad bowl.
2. In I bowl, whisk the balsamic vinegar with olive oil, salt, and crushed pepper.
3. Pour the vinegar oil dressing over the salad and toss gently to coat.
4. Serve the Mediterranean Melon and Prosciutto Salad immediately.

Nutritions

Calories: 150 , Fat: 8g , Protein: 9g , Carbohydrate: 10g

PREPARATION TIME: 10 MIN

COOKING TIME: 0 MIN

SERVINGS: 2

GREEK-STYLE FRUIT AND NUT PLATTER WITH HONEY AND YOGURT DIP

Ingredients

- 2 cups mixed fresh fruits (such as grapes, berries, and sliced melon)
- 1/2 cup mixed nuts (such as almonds, walnuts, and pistachios)
- 1/2 cup Greek yogurt
- 2 tablespoons honey

Directions

1. Arrange the mixed fresh fruits and mixed nuts on a platter.
2. Combine the Greek yogurt and honey in a small bowl to make the dip.
3. Serve the Greek-Style Fruit and Nut Platter with the honey-yogurt dip on the side.

Nutritions

Calories: 180 , Fat: 10g , Protein: 6g , Carbohydrate: 20g

PREPARATION TIME: 10 MIN

COOKING TIME: 0 MIN

SERVINGS: 2

MEDITERRANEAN ORANGE AND DATE SALAD

Ingredients

- 2 oranges, peeled and sliced
- 1/2 cup pitted dates, chopped
- 1/4 cup chopped walnuts
- 2 tablespoons orange juice
- 1 tablespoon extra-virgin olive oil
- Salt to taste

Directions

1. Combine the orange slices, chopped dates, and chopped walnuts in a salad bowl.
2. Whisk the orange juice with olive oil and salt in a small bowl.
3. Drizzle the orange juice & oil dressing over the salad and toss gently to coat.
4. Serve the Mediterranean Orange and Date Salad immediately.

Nutritions

Calories: 200 , Fat: 10g , Protein: 2g , Carbohydrate: 30g

PREPARATION TIME: 10 MIN

COOKING TIME: 0 MIN

SERVINGS: 2

GREEK-STYLE STUFFED PEACHES WITH HONEY AND RICOTTA

Ingredients

- 2 ripe peaches, halved and pitted
- 1/4 cup ricotta cheese
- 2 tablespoons honey
- 2 tablespoons chopped pistachios

Directions

1. Put the peach halves, cut side up, on a serving plate.
2. Fill each peach half with ricotta cheese.
3. Drizzle the honey over the stuffed peaches.
4. Sprinkle with chopped pistachios.
5. Serve the Greek-Style Stuffed Peaches immediately.

Nutritions

Calories: 180 , Fat: 6g, Protein: 6g , Carbohydrate: 30g

PREPARATION TIME: 10 MIN

COOKING TIME: 0 MIN

SERVINGS: 2

Chapter 12:

10 Mediterranean Snack Recipes

GREEK-STYLE HUMMUS WITH PITA BREAD

Ingredients

- 1 can (15 oz weight) chickpeas, drained and rinsed
- 2 tablespoons tahini
- 2 tablespoons fresh lemon juice
- 2 cloves garlic, minced
- 1/4 teaspoon ground cumin
- 2 tablespoons extra-virgin olive oil
- Salt and pepper to taste
- Pita bread for serving

Directions

1. Combine chickpeas, tahini, lemon juice, minced garlic, ground cumin, extra-virgin olive oil, salt, and pepper in a food blender. Process until smooth and creamy.
2. Serve the hummus with pita bread for dipping.

Nutritions

Calories: 160 , Fat: 8g , Protein: 6g , Carbohydrate: 18g

PREPARATION TIME: 10 MIN

COOKING TIME: 0 MIN

SERVINGS: 4

MEDITERRANEAN CUCUMBER AND TOMATO BITES

Ingredients

- 1 English cucumber
- 2 medium tomatoes
- 1/4 cup crumbled feta cheese
- 1 tablespoon chopped fresh dill
- 1 tablespoon extra-virgin olive oil
- Salt and pepper to taste

Directions

1. Slice the cucumber and tomatoes into rounds. Arrange the cucumber and tomato slices on a platter.
2. Sprinkle with crumbled feta cheese and chopped fresh dill. Drizzle with extra-virgin olive oil. Powder it with salt and pepper. Serve the cucumber and tomato bites as a refreshing snack.

Nutritions

Calories: 60 , Fat: 4g , Protein: 2g , Carbohydrate: 4g

PREPARATION TIME: 10 MIN

COOKING TIME: 0 MIN

SERVINGS: 4

STUFFED GRAPE LEAVES (DOLMADES)

Ingredients

- 1 jar (8 ounces) of grape leaves in brine
- 1 cup cooked long-grain rice
- 1/2 cup chopped fresh dill
- 1/4 cup chopped fresh mint
- 1/4 cup chopped fresh parsley
- 1/4 cup lemon juice
- 2 tablespoons extra-virgin olive oil
- Salt and pepper to taste

Directions

1. Rinse the grape leaves under cold water and remove any stems. Mix the cooked rice in a bowl with chopped fresh dill, chopped fresh mint, chopped fresh parsley, lemon juice, extra-virgin olive oil, salt, and pepper.
2. Place a grape leaf on the smooth surface, shiny side down. Spoon about 1 tablespoon of the rice mixture onto the center of the grape leaf.
3. Fold the sides of the grape leaf over the filling and roll it up tightly. Repeat with the leftover grape leaves and filling. Place the stuffed grape leaves in a saucepan and cover with water.
4. Take a boil, decrease the stove heat, and simmer for 30 minutes. Drain the stuffed grape leaves and let them cool before serving.

Nutritions

Calories: 140 , Fat: 6g , Protein: 2g, Carbohydrate: 20g

PREPARATION TIME: 30 MIN

COOKING TIME: 30 MIN

SERVINGS: 4

MEDITERRANEAN OLIVE AND FETA SKEWERS

Ingredients

- 1 cup mixed olives (Kalamata, green, etc.)
- 1/2 cup cherry tomatoes
- 1/2 cup cubed feta cheese
- 1 tablespoon extra-virgin olive oil
- 1 tablespoon chopped fresh parsley
- Salt and pepper to taste
- Skewers

Directions

1. Thread the olives, cherry tomatoes, and feta cheese onto skewers. Drizzle with extra-virgin olive oil.
2. Sprinkle with chopped fresh parsley. Powder it with salt and crushed pepper. Serve the olive and feta skewers as a flavorful snack.

Nutritions

Calories: 120 , Fat: 10g , Protein: 4g , Carbohydrate: 4g

PREPARATION TIME: 15 MIN

COOKING TIME: 0 MIN

SERVINGS: 4

GREEK TZATZIKI WITH FRESH VEGETABLES

Ingredients

- 1 cucumber
- 1 cup Greek yogurt
- 2 cloves garlic, minced
- 1 tablespoon extra-virgin olive oil
- 1 tablespoon chopped fresh dill
- 1 tablespoon fresh lemon juice
- Salt and pepper to taste
- Fresh vegetables (carrot sticks, celery sticks, cherry tomatoes) for se

Directions

1. Grate the cucumber to squeeze out the excess liquid. Combine the grated cucumber, Greek yogurt, minced garlic, extra-virgin olive oil, chopped fresh dill, lemon juice, salt, and pepper in a bowl.
2. Stir well to combine. Serve the tzatziki with fresh vegetables for dipping.

Nutritions

Calories: 70 , Fat: 4g , Protein: 5g, Carbohydrate: 4g

PREPARATION TIME: 15 MIN

COOKING TIME: 0 MIN

SERVINGS: 4

GREEK-STYLE BAKED FETA WITH HONEY AND SESAME SEEDS

Ingredients

- 1 block (8 ounces) of feta cheese
- 2 tablespoons honey
- 1 tablespoon sesame seeds

Directions

1. Set the oven heat to 400°F (200°C). Place the block of feta cheese on a baking dish. Drizzle the honey over the feta cheese.
2. Sprinkle the sesame seeds on top. Bake for 10 minutes or until the feta cheese softens and the sesame seeds turn golden. Serve the baked feta with bread or crackers.

Nutritions

Calories: 180 , Fat: 12g , Protein: 10g , Carbohydrate: 10g

PREPARATION TIME: 5 MIN

COOKING TIME: 10 MIN

SERVINGS: 4

CHICKPEA AND OLIVE BRUSCHETTA

Ingredients

- 1 can (15 ounces) chickpeas, drained and rinsed
- 1/2 cup pitted Kalamata olives, chopped
- 1/4 cup chopped fresh parsley
- 2 tablespoons extra-virgin olive oil
- 1 tablespoon lemon juice
- 1 garlic clove, minced
- Salt and pepper to taste
- Baguette slices toasted

Directions

1. Combine the chickpeas, chopped Kalamata olives, chopped fresh parsley, extra-virgin olive oil, lemon juice, minced garlic, salt, and pepper in a bowl. Mix well to combine.
2. Spoon the chickpea and olive mixture onto the toasted baguette slices. Serve the Mediterranean chickpea and olive bruschetta as a tasty appetizer or snack.

Nutritions

Calories: 200 , Fat: 10g , Protein: 6g , Carbohydrate: 22g

PREPARATION TIME: 15 MIN

COOKING TIME: 5 MIN

SERVINGS: 4

MEDITERRANEAN ROASTED CHICKPEAS

Ingredients

- 2 cans (15 ounces each) of chickpeas, drained and rinsed
- 2 tablespoons extra-virgin olive oil
- 1 teaspoon ground cumin
- 1 teaspoon paprika
- 1/2 teaspoon garlic powder
- 1/2 teaspoon salt
- 1/4 teaspoon cayenne pepper (optional)

Directions

1. Set the oven heat to 400°F (200°C). Mix the chickpeas with the extra-virgin olive oil, ground cumin, paprika, garlic powder, salt, and cayenne pepper (if using).
2. Spread the seasoned chickpeas in one layer on a baking sheet. Roast in the oven for 37-40 minutes or until crispy and golden brown. Allow the roasted chickpeas to cool before serving.

Nutritions

Calories: 200 , Fat: 6g , Protein: 9g , Carbohydrate: 29g

PREPARATION TIME: 5 MIN

COOKING TIME: 40 MIN

SERVINGS: 4

GREEK-STYLE BAKED ZUCCHINI CHIPS

Ingredients

- 2 zucchini, sliced into thin rounds
- 2 tablespoons extra-virgin olive oil
- 1/4 cup grated Parmesan cheese
- 1/2 teaspoon dried oregano
- 1/2 teaspoon garlic powder
- Salt and pepper to taste

Directions

1. Set the oven heat to 425°F (220°C). Toss the zucchini slices with the extra-virgin olive oil, grated Parmesan cheese, dried oregano, garlic powder, salt, and pepper in a bowl.
2. Arrange the coated zucchini slices in one layer on a baking sheet.
3. Bake for 23-25 minutes or until the zucchini chips are crispy and golden brown. Let the baked zucchini chips cool slightly before serving.

Nutritions

Calories: 100 , Fat: 7g , Protein: 3g , Carbohydrate: 7g

PREPARATION TIME: 10 MIN

COOKING TIME: 25 MIN

SERVINGS: 4

DATES STUFFED WITH CHEESE AND ALMONDS

Ingredients

- 8 Medjool dates, pitted
- 4 ounces of goat cheese
- 1/4 cup chopped almonds

Directions

1. Gently open each pitted date with a small amount of goat cheese. Press chopped almonds onto the goat cheese to adhere.
2. Repeat with the leftover dates. Serve the stuffed dates as a sweet and savory snack.

Nutritions

Calories: 180 , Fat: 6g , Protein: 5g , Carbohydrate: 30g

PREPARATION TIME: 10 MIN

COOKING TIME: 0 MIN

SERVINGS: 4

Chapter 13:

10 Mediterranean Dessert Recipes

MEDITERRANEAN ORANGE AND ALMOND CAKE

Ingredients

- 2 oranges
- 4 eggs
- 1 cup almond flour
- 1/2 cup honey
- 1 teaspoon baking powder
- 1/4 teaspoon salt
- Sliced almonds for garnish

Directions

1. Set the oven heat to 350°F (180°C) and grease a round cake pan. Boil the oranges in a saucepan for 1 hour. Drain and let them cool.
2. Cut the oranges into quarters, remove the seeds, and place them in a blender or food processor. Blend until smooth.
3. In a bowl, beat the eggs with honey together until well combined. Add orange puree, almond flour, baking powder, and salt. Stir until all are well mixed.
4. Pour the batter into the prepared round cake pan and smooth the top.
5. Bake for 37-40 minutes. Then remove and cool the cake before removing it from the pan. Garnish with sliced almonds before serving.

Nutritions

Calories: 190 , Fat: 8g , Protein: 6g , Carbohydrate: 25g

PREPARATION TIME: 15 MIN

COOKING TIME: 40 MIN

SERVINGS: 8

GREEK YOGURT WITH HONEY AND PISTACHIOS

Ingredients

- ½ cup Greek yogurt
- 1 tablespoon honey
- 1 tablespoon chopped pistachios

Directions

1. Grab the serving bowl, and spoon the Greek yogurt into the serving bowl. Drop the honey all over the yogurt and sprinkle the chopped pistachios on top of the drizzled honey. Mix well before eating.

Nutritions

Calories: 180 , Fat: 5g , Protein: 12g , Carbohydrate: 25g

PREPARATION TIME: 5 MIN

COOKING TIME: 0 MIN

SERVINGS: 1

LEMON AND OLIVE OIL CAKE

Ingredients

- 1½ cups almond flour
- ½ cup coconut flour
- ½ cup honey
- ¼ cup olive oil
- 4 eggs
- Zest of 1 lemon
- Juice of 1 lemon
- 1 teaspoon baking powder
- 1/4 teaspoon salt

Directions

1. Set the oven heat to 350°F (180°C) and grease a cake pan. Whisk the almond flour, coconut flour, baking powder, and salt in a bowl. In the other bowl, beat the eggs with honey, olive oil, lemon zest, and lemon juice until well combined.
2. Gradually add the dry elements to the wet, stirring until the batter is smooth. Pour the batter into the already greased cake pan and smooth the top. Bake for 31-35 minutes. Allow the cake to cool before serving.

Nutritions

Calories: 220 , Fat: 15g , Protein: 6g , Carbohydrate: 17g

PREPARATION TIME: 15 MIN

COOKING TIME: 35 MIN

SERVINGS: 8

POMEGRANATE AND PISTACHIO SEMOLINA CAKE

Ingredients

- 1 cup semolina flour
- 1/2 cup almond flour
- 1/2 cup honey
- 1/4 cup olive oil
- 1 cup plain Greek yogurt
- 1/2 cup pomegranate arils
- 1/4 cup chopped pistachios
- 1 teaspoon baking powder
- 1/4 teaspoon salt

Directions

1. Set the oven heat to 350°F (180°C) and grease a cake pan. Combine the semolina flour, almond flour, baking powder, and salt in a bowl. Whisk the honey, olive oil, and Greek yogurt in the other bowl.
2. Gradually add the dry elements to the wet, mixing until well combined. Fold in the pomegranate arils and chopped pistachios. Pour the batter into the greased round cake pan and smooth the top.
3. Bake for 43-45 minutes or until the cake is golden brown. Allow the cake to cool before serving.

Nutritions

Calories: 250 , Fat: 12g , Protein: 6g , Carbohydrate: 30g

PREPARATION TIME: 20 MIN

COOKING TIME: 45 MIN

SERVINGS: 8

GREEK LOUKOUMADES (HONEY AND CINNAMON DOUGHNUTS)

Ingredients

- 2 cups all-purpose flour
- 1 tablespoon honey
- 1 teaspoon active dry yeast
- 1/4 teaspoon salt
- 1 cup lukewarm water
- Vegetable oil for frying
- Honey and ground cinnamon for drizzling

Directions

1. Dissolve the yeast in hot water in a small bowl and let it sit for 5 minutes or until
2. it becomes foamy.
3. Mix the flour with salt together in a big bowl. In the middle, make a well and pour the yeast mixture and honey into it.
4. Stir until all are well mixed and the mixture is smooth.
5. Let the batter rise for an hour in a warm place
6. while the bowl is covered with a clean cooking towel.
7. Heat vegetable oil to 350°F (180°C) in a deep pot.
8. Using a tablespoon, scoop small portions of the batter and drop them gently into the hot oil. Fry until golden brown, turning them occasionally to ensure even cooking.
9. Remove the loukoumades and drain them on paper towels.
10. Drizzle the honey, then spread with ground cinnamon before serving.

Nutritions

Calories: 180 , Fat: 2g , Protein: 4g , Carbohydrate: 37g

PREPARATION TIME: 20 MIN

COOKING TIME: 20 MIN

SERVINGS: 8

MEDITERRANEAN APRICOT AND ALMOND TART

Ingredients

- 1 sheet frozen puff pastry, thawed
- 1/2 cup almond flour
- 1/4 cup honey
- 1/4 cup almond milk
- 1 teaspoon almond extract
- 8 apricots, halved and pitted
- Sliced almonds for garnish

Directions

1. Set the oven heat to 375°F (190°C) and line a tart pan with parchment paper. Roll out the puff pastry until it can fit the tart pan and press it into it, trimming any excess.
2. Whisk the almond flour with honey, almond milk, and almond extract until well combined. Spread the almond mixture evenly over the puff pastry. Press the apricot halves on the almond mixture, and cut the side down.
3. Sprinkle sliced almonds over the apricots. Bake for 23-25 minutes or until the pastry is golden brown and the apricots are tender.
4. Let the tart cool before serving.

Nutritions

Calories: 220 , Fat: 10g , Protein: 4g , Carbohydrate: 30g

PREPARATION TIME: 15 MIN

COOKING TIME: 28 MIN

SERVINGS: 8

MEDITERRANEAN PEAR AND ALMOND TART

Ingredients

- 1 sheet frozen puff pastry, thawed
- 2 ripe pears, peeled, cored, and sliced
- ½ cup almond flour
- ¼ cup honey
- ¼ cup almond milk
- 1 teaspoon almond extract
- Sliced almonds for garnish

Directions

1. Roll out the puff pastry sheet until it fits into the tart pan and press it into it, trimming any excess.
2. Whisk the almond flour with honey, almond milk, and almond extract until well combined. Spread the almond mixture evenly over the puff pastry.
3. Spread and press the sliced pears on top of the almond mixture. Sprinkle sliced almonds over the pears.
4. Bake for 31-35 minutes until the pastry is golden brown and the pears are tender.
5. Let the tart cool before serving.

Nutritions

Calories: 230 , Fat: 10g , Protein: 4g , Carbohydrate: 32g

PREPARATION TIME: 20 MIN

COOKING TIME: 35 MIN

SERVINGS: 8

LEMON AND ROSEWATER SORBET

Ingredients

- 1 cup fresh lemon juice
- 1 cup water
- ½ cup honey
- 1 teaspoon rosewater
- Lemon zest for garnish

Directions

1. Combine the lemon juice, water, honey, and rosewater in a bowl. Whisk the mixture until the honey is completely dissolved after pouring the liquid into an ice cream maker, churn as per the instructions provided by the manufacturer.
2. Place the sorbet in a container with a lid and place it in the freezer for at least four hours or until it has reached the desired consistency.
3. Scoop the sorbet into bowls or glasses and garnish with lemon zest before serving.

Nutritions

Calories: 110 , Fat: 0g , Protein: 0g , Carbohydrate: 29g

PREPARATION TIME: 10 MIN

COOKING TIME: 0 MIN

SERVINGS: 4

GREEK SEMOLINA PUDDING WITH CINNAMON AND RAISINS

Ingredients

- 1 cup semolina flour
- ½ cup honey
- ¼ cup olive oil
- 2 cups water
- ½ cup raisins
- 1 teaspoon ground cinnamon
- Chopped almonds for garnish

Directions

1. In a saucepan, heat ¼ cup oil over medium heat. Add the semolina flour and cook, stirring constantly, for about 5 minutes or until the semolina turns golden brown. In the other saucepan, heat the water and honey until the honey is dissolved.
2. Slowly pour the honey-water mixture into the semolina mixture, stirring regularly to prevent lumps from forming. Add raisins and ground cinnamon to the mixture and continue stirring for 5 minutes or until the halva thickens and pulls away from the sides of the pan.
3. Remove the halva from the heat and let it cool for a few minutes. Scoop the halva into individual serving bowls or molds and press it down gently to shape it. Let the halva cool completely and refrigerate for two hours (at least) to set. Garnish with chopped almonds before serving.

Nutritions

Calories: 220 , Fat: 8g , Protein: 3g , Carbohydrate: 35g

PREPARATION TIME: 10 MIN

COOKING TIME: 20 MIN

SERVINGS: 8

MEDITERRANEAN CHOCOLATE AND FIG TART

Ingredients

- 1 sheet frozen puff pastry, thawed
- ½ cup dark chocolate, chopped
- ¼ cup almond flour
- ¼ cup honey
- 8 fresh figs, quartered
- Chopped pistachios for garnish

Directions

1. Set the oven heat to 375°F (190°C) and arrange the tart pan with parchment paper. Roll out the puff pastry sheet until it can fit the tart pan and press it into it, trimming any excess. In a microwave, melt the dark chocolate briefly, stirring in between, until smooth.
2. In a bowl, whisk the almond flour with honey. Add melted chocolate until well combined. Spread the chocolate mixture evenly over the puff pastry. Arrange the quartered figs on top of the chocolate mixture.
3. Bake for 23-25 minutes or until the pastry is golden brown and the figs are tender. Garnish with chopped pistachios before serving.

Nutritions

Calories: 260, Fat: 14g , Protein: 4g , Carbohydrate: 34

PREPARATION TIME: 20 MIN

COOKING TIME: 25 MIN

SERVINGS: 8

CONCLUSION

Embracing the Mediterranean diet is more than a mere dietary choice; it's an introduction to a vibrant culture, a healthier lifestyle, and a fresh perspective on what it truly means to enjoy food. It's about eating whole, nutritious, simple foods, indulging occasionally, and making mealtime an enjoyable social event.

The principles of the Mediterranean diet stand on the pillars of balance, variety, and moderation. Its cornerstone is a plethora of plant-based foods, heart-healthy fats such as olive oil, lean proteins, and an array of aromatic herbs and spices. On the other hand, it limits red meat, processed foods, and foods high in refined sugar. These concepts combine to offer a diet high in fiber, antioxidants, and unsaturated fats. This diet contributes to improved digestive health, heart health, and decreased chance of developing chronic diseases.

As you move forward on this culinary journey, here are a few tips to continue following the Mediterranean diet:

- Emphasize Fruits and Vegetables: Aim for at least five daily servings of fresh, frozen, or tinned fruits and vegetables. They provide valuable nutrients and fiber.
- Choose Whole Grains: Opt for whole-grain bread, pasta, and rice whenever possible. They provide more nutrients and keep you feeling full longer.
- Lean Towards Lean Proteins: Go for lean protein sources such as poultry, fish, and legumes. Reserve red meat for the occasional indulgence.
- Savor Seafood: Aim for at least two servings of seafood each week. Seafood is rich in omega-3 heart-healthy fatty acids.
- Use Olive Oil: Swap butter and other fats for olive oil, a healthier, more flavorful option.
- Spice it Up: Use herbs and spices to add flavor without extra sodium or fat.
- Stay Active: The Mediterranean lifestyle also includes regular physical activity. It can be as simple as a daily walk or as rigorous as a workout session.

Remember, the Mediterranean diet isn't about strict rules or deprivation. It's about nourishing your body with nutritious food, enjoying meals with family and friends, and maintaining a balanced lifestyle. With its focus on whole foods, fresh flavors, and healthy fats, the Mediterranean diet offers a practical and enjoyable way to enhance health and savor the joy of good food.
Thank you for joining this journey through the Mediterranean Diet. Enjoy the process, enjoy the food, and most importantly, enjoy the newfound health and vitality that comes from adopting one of the most beneficial dietary regimes in the world. Bon appétit!

60 DAYS SHOPPING LIST

Day	Ingredients	Quantities
Day 1		
	Quinoa Breakfast Bowl with Berries and Nuts	
	Quinoa	2 cups
	Mixed Berries	2 cups
	Mixed Nuts	1 cup
	Honey or Sweetener of choice	4 tablespoons
	Milk or Dairy-free alternative	To serve
	Mediterranean Beef and Vegetable Stir-fry	
	Beef Steak	500 grams
	Mixed Vegetables (like bell peppers, zucchini, cherry tomatoes)	2 cups
	Olive oil	2 tablespoons
	Garlic	2 cloves
	Herbs and Spices	To taste
	Grilled Salmon with Lemon and Dill	
	Salmon Fillets	2 pieces
	Lemon	1 whole
	Fresh Dill	A handful
	Olive oil	2 tablespoons
	Salt and Pepper	To taste
	Greek-Style Hummus with Pita Bread	
	Chickpeas (canned or soaked and boiled)	2 cups
	Tahini	4 tablespoons
	Lemon Juice	2 tablespoons
	Garlic	2 cloves
	Olive oil	4 tablespoons
	Pita Bread	4 pieces
Day 2		
	Veggie and Whole Grain Scramble	
	Whole Grains (like brown rice or quinoa)	2 cups
	Mixed Vegetables (like bell peppers, onions, tomatoes)	3 cups
	Eggs	4 large
	Olive oil	2 tablespoons
	Salt and Pepper	To taste
	Beef Tagine with Olives and Preserved Lemon	
	Beef Cubes	500 grams
	Green Olives	1 cup
	Preserved Lemon	1 whole
	Garlic	2 cloves

	Olive oil	2 tablespoons
	Moroccan spices (like cumin, coriander, turmeric, cinnamon)	To taste
	Greek-style Shrimp with Tomatoes and Feta	
	Shrimp	500 grams
	Cherry Tomatoes	2 cups
	Feta Cheese	200 grams
	Garlic	2 cloves
	Olive oil	2 tablespoons
	Herbs (like oregano and dill)	To taste
	Mediterranean Cucumber and Tomato Bites	
	Cucumber	1 large
	Cherry Tomatoes	1 cup
	Feta Cheese	200 grams
	Olive oil	To drizzle
	Salt and Pepper	To taste
Day 3		
	Buckwheat Pancakes with Fresh Berries	
	Buckwheat Flour	2 cups
	Fresh Berries	2 cups
	Eggs	2 large
	Milk	1 cup
	Baking Powder	1 tablespoon
	Honey or Sweetener of choice	To taste
Day 4		
	Whole Rye Toast with Avocado and Tomato	
	Whole Rye Bread	4 slices
	Avocados	2 medium
	Tomatoes	2 medium
	Salt and Pepper	To taste
Day 5		
	Warm Barley and Berry Breakfast	
	Barley	2 cups
	Fresh Berries	2 cups
	Honey or Sweetener of choice	To taste
	Milk or Dairy-free alternative	To serve
Day 6		
	Chia and Quinoa Pudding with Fresh Fruits	
	Chia Seeds	1/2 cup
	Quinoa	1 cup
	Fresh Fruits	2 cups
	Honey or Sweetener of choice	To taste
	Milk or Dairy-free alternative	To serve
Day 7		

	Whole Grain Blueberry Muffins	
	Whole Grain Flour	2 cups
	Blueberries	2 cups
	Eggs	2 large
	Milk	1 cup
	Baking Powder	1 tablespoon
	Honey or Sweetener of choice	To taste
Day 8		
	Millet Porridge with Cinnamon Apples	
	Millet	1 cup
	Apples	2 medium
	Cinnamon	1 teaspoon
	Milk or Dairy-free alternative	2 cups
	Honey or Sweetener of choice	To taste
Day 9		
	Buckwheat Crepes with Spinach and Feta	
	Buckwheat Flour	2 cups
	Eggs	2 large
	Milk	1 cup
	Spinach	2 cups
	Feta Cheese	200 grams
Day 10		
	Whole Grain Tacos with Avocado and Beans	
	Whole Grain Tortillas	8 small
	Avocados	2 medium
	Black Beans	1 can
	Tomatoes	2 medium
	Cheese of choice	200 grams
Day 11		
	Bulgur Wheat Porridge with Raisins and Almonds	
	Bulgur Wheat	1 cup
	Raisins	1/2 cup
	Almonds	1/2 cup
	Milk or Dairy-free alternative	2 cups
	Honey or Sweetener of choice	To taste
Day 12		
	Toast with Nut Butter and Banana	
	Bread of choice	4 slices
	Nut Butter of choice	4 tablespoons
	Bananas	2 medium
Day 13		
	Millet and Berry Smoothie Bowl	
	Millet	1/2 cup

	Fresh Berries	2 cups
	Banana	1 medium
	Milk or Dairy-free alternative	1 cup
	Honey or Sweetener of choice	To taste
Day 14		
	Apple Cinnamon Whole Grain Pancakes	
	Whole Grain Flour	2 cups
	Apples	2 medium
	Eggs	2 large
	Milk	1 cup
	Baking Powder	1 tablespoon
	Honey or Sweetener of choice	To taste
	Cinnamon	1 teaspoon
Day 15		
	Mediterranean Burritos with Tomato and Cheese	
	Whole Grain Tortillas	8 small
	Tomatoes	2 medium
	Cheese of choice	200 grams
	Avocados	2 medium
	Black Beans	1 can
Day 16		
	Savory Oatmeal with Sauteed Vegetables	
	Oats	2 cups
	Mixed Vegetables of choice (for sauteing)	2 cups
	Olive Oil	2 tablespoons
	Salt and Pepper	To taste
Day 17		
	Overnight Chia Pudding with Quinoa and Berries	
	Chia Seeds	1/2 cup
	Quinoa	1 cup
	Fresh Berries	2 cups
	Milk or Dairy-free alternative	To serve
	Honey or Sweetener of choice	To taste
Day 18		
	Rye Bread with Smashed Avocado and Poached Egg	
	Rye Bread	4 slices
	Avocados	2 medium
	Eggs	4 large
	Salt and Pepper	To taste
Day 19		
	Greek Yogurt with Honey and Fresh Berries	
	Greek Yogurt	2 cups
	Honey	To taste

	Fresh Berries	2 cups
Day 20		
	Mediterranean Fig and Goat Cheese Salad	
	Figs	8 fresh
	Goat Cheese	200 grams
	Mixed Salad Greens	4 cups
	Honey	2 tablespoons
	Olive Oil	4 tablespoons
Day 21		
	Greek-Style Baked Apples with Honey and Walnuts	
	Apples	2
	Honey	4 tbsp
	Walnuts	1/2 cup
Day 22		
	Mediterranean Citrus and Olive Salad	
	Citrus fruits (e.g., oranges, grapefruit)	4
	Olives	1/2 cup
	Olive oil	2 tbsp
Day 23		
	Grilled Peach and Mozzarella Salad	
	Peaches	4
	Mozzarella	200g
	Mixed salad greens	4 cups
Day 24		
	Mediterranean Pear and Arugula Salad with Feta	
	Pears	2
	Arugula	4 cups
	Feta cheese	200g
Day 25		
	Greek Yogurt Parfait with Fresh Fruits and Honey	
	Greek yogurt	2 cups
	Fresh fruits	2 cups
	Honey	4 tbsp
Day 26		
	Mediterranean Avocado and Strawberry Salad	
	Avocado	2
	Strawberries	1 cup
	Mixed salad greens	4 cups
Day 27		
	Mediterranean Citrus and Fennel Salad	
	Citrus fruits (e.g., oranges, grapefruit)	4
	Fennel bulb	1
	Olive oil	2 tbsp

Day 28		
	Mediterranean Apple and Cabbage Slaw	
	Apples	2
	Cabbage	1/2 head
	Carrots	2
	Vinegar	2 tbsp
Day 29		
	Greek-Style Cherry Tomato and Watermelon Salad	
	Cherry tomatoes	1 cup
	Watermelon	1/4 medium
	Feta cheese	200g
Day 30		
	Mediterranean Fruit Salad with Lemon Mint Dressing	
	Mixed fruits (berries, melon, etc.)	4 cups
	Lemon	1
	Fresh mint leaves	A handful
Day 31		
	Millet Porridge with Cinnamon Apples	
	Millet	1 cup
	Apples	2
	Cinnamon	1 tsp
	Chicken Tagine with Olives and Preserved Lemon	
	Chicken	500g
	Olives	1/2 cup
	Preserved lemons	2
	Grilled Scallops with Garlic and Herbs	
	Scallops	500g
	Garlic	2 cloves
	Fresh herbs	A handful
	Greek Semolina Pudding with Cinnamon and Raisins	
	Semolina	1 cup
	Cinnamon	1 tsp
	Raisins	1/2 cup
Day 32		
	Overnight Chia Pudding with Quinoa and Berries	
	Chia seeds	1/4 cup
	Quinoa	1/2 cup
	Mixed berries	1 cup
	Roasted Pork Tenderloin with Olives and Capers	
	Pork tenderloin	500g
	Olives	1/2 cup
	Capers	2 tbsp
	Quinoa and White Bean Stew	

	Quinoa	1 cup
	White beans	1 can
	Vegetables for stew	To taste
	Dates Stuffed with Cheese and Almonds	
	Dates	10
	Cheese	100g
	Almonds	10
Day 33		
	Mediterranean Burritos with Tomato and Cheese	
	Burrito wraps	2
	Tomatoes	1
	Cheese	1/2 cup
	Mediterranean Lamb and Vegetable Skewers	
	Lamb meat	500g
	Mixed vegetables for skewers	To taste
	Baked Trout with Lemon and Thyme	
	Trout fillet	2
	Lemon	1
	Thyme	1 tbsp
	Mediterranean Chocolate and Fig Tart	
	Dark chocolate	100g
	Figs	4
	Pie crust	1
Day 34		
	Rye Bread with Smashed Avocado and Poached Egg	
	Rye bread	2 slices
	Avocado	1
	Egg	1
	Turkey Meatballs with Tomato and Basil Sauce	
	Ground turkey	500g
	Tomatoes	2
	Basil	To taste
	Greek-Style Baked Chickpeas with Tomato	
	Chickpeas	1 can
	Tomatoes	2
	Greek-Style Hummus with Pita Bread	
	Chickpeas	1 can
	Tahini	2 tbsp
	Pita bread	4
Day 35		
	Buckwheat Crepes with Spinach and Feta	
	Buckwheat flour	2 cups
	Spinach	1 cup

	Feta cheese	1/2 cup
	Chicken Paella with Saffron and Olives	
	Chicken thighs	500g
	Paella rice	2 cups
	Saffron	A pinch
	Olives	1 cup
	Mediterranean-style Fish Tacos	
	Fish fillets	2
	Tortillas	4
	Taco fillings (lettuce, tomato, etc.)	To taste
	Lemon and Olive Oil Cake	
	Lemons	2
	Olive oil	1 cup
	Flour	2 cups
	Sugar	1 cup
Day 36		
	Toast with Nut Butter and Banana	
	Bread	2 slices
	Nut butter	2 tbsp
	Banana	1
	Mediterranean Beef and Vegetable Stir-fry	
	Beef	500g
	Mixed vegetables	To taste
	Greek Lentil Soup (Fakes)	
	Lentils	1 cup
	Onion	1
	Garlic	2 cloves
	Greek Yogurt with Honey and Pistachios	
	Greek yogurt	2 cups
	Honey	2 tbsp
	Pistachios	1/4 cup
Day 37		
	Whole Grain Tacos with Avocado and Beans	
	Whole grain tortillas	2
	Avocado	1
	Beans	1 cup
	Grilled Pork Chops with Lemon and Oregano	
	Pork chops	2
	Lemon	1
	Oregano	1 tsp
	Sea Bass with Mediterranean Salsa	
	Sea bass fillets	2
	Salsa ingredients (tomato, onion, etc.)	To taste

	Mediterranean Pear and Almond Tart	
	Pears	2
	Almonds	1/2 cup
	Tart crust	1
Day 38		
	Millet and Berry Smoothie Bowl	
	Millet	1/4 cup
	Berries	1 cup
	Mediterranean Pork and Bean Stew	
	Pork	500g
	Beans	1 cup
	Shrimp and Couscous with Feta	
	Shrimp	500g
	Couscous	1 cup
	Feta cheese	1/2 cup
	Mediterranean Orange and Almond Cake	
	Oranges	2
	Almonds	1 cup
	Cake ingredients (flour, sugar, etc.)	To taste
Day 39		
	Quinoa and Vegetable Breakfast Hash	
	Quinoa	1 cup
	Mixed vegetables	2 cups
	Beef Tagine with Olives and Preserved Lemon	
	Beef	1 pound
	Olives	1 cup
	Preserved lemon	1
	Greek-Style Lentil and Tomato Stew	
	Lentils	1 cup
	Tomatoes	2 cups
	Pomegranate and Pistachio Semolina Cake	
	Pomegranate seeds	1/2 cup
	Pistachios	1/2 cup
	Semolina	1 cup
Day 40		
	Whole Grain Blueberry Muffins	
	Whole grain muffin mix	1 packet
	Blueberries	1 cup
	Mediterranean Chicken and Vegetable Stir-fry	
	Chicken	1 pound
	Mixed vegetables	2 cups
	Mediterranean Fish Stew with Garlic and Saffron	
	Mixed fish (cod, haddock, etc.)	1 pound

	Garlic	4 cloves
	Saffron	1 pinch
	Lemon and Rosewater Sorbet	
	Lemons	3
	Rosewater	2 tablespoons
Day 41		
	Apple Cinnamon Whole Grain Pancakes	
	Whole grain pancake mix	1 packet
	Apples	2
	Cinnamon	1 teaspoon
	Grilled Turkey Skewers with Garlic and Herbs	
	Turkey breast	1 pound
	Garlic	4 cloves
	Fresh herbs	A handful
	Greek-Style Lentil and Spinach Soup	
	Lentils	1 cup
	Spinach	2 cups
	Greek Loukoumades (Honey and Cinnamon Doughnuts)	
	Flour	2 cups
	Yeast	2 teaspoons
	Honey	1 cup
	Cinnamon	1 teaspoon
Day 42		
	Buckwheat Pancakes with Fresh Berries	
	Buckwheat flour	1 cup
	Fresh berries	1 cup
	Mediterranean Lamb and Barley Stew	
	Lamb	1 pound
	Barley	1 cup
	Baked Haddock with Olives and Tomatoes	
	Haddock fillets	2
	Olives	1/2 cup
	Tomatoes	2
	Mediterranean Apricot and Almond Tart	
	Apricots	8
	Almonds	1/2 cup
	Tart crust	1
Day 43		
	Warm Barley and Berry Breakfast	
	Barley	1 cup
	Mixed berries	1 cup
	Turkey and Vegetable Stuffed Peppers	
	Bell peppers	4

	Ground turkey	1 pound
	Mixed vegetables	2 cups
	Barley and Chickpea Soup	
	Barley	1 cup
	Chickpeas	1 can
	Greek-Style Hummus with Pita Bread	
	Chickpeas	1 can
	Tahini	2 tablespoons
	Pita bread	4
Day 44		
	Veggie and Whole Grain Scramble	
	Whole grain bread	2 slices
	Mixed vegetables	To taste
	Eggs	4
	Mediterranean Beef Stuffed Bell Peppers	
	Bell peppers	4
	Ground beef	1 pound
	Rice	1/2 cup
	Grilled Tuna Steaks with Caper Vinaigrette	
	Tuna steaks	2
	Capers	2 tablespoons
	Vinegar	2 tablespoons
	Dates Stuffed with Cheese and Almonds	
	Dates	8
	Cheese (such as goat cheese or cream cheese)	4 ounces
	Almonds	8
Day 45		
	Savory Oatmeal with Sautéed Vegetables	
	Oats	1 cup
	Mixed vegetables	To taste
	Mediterranean Chicken and Orzo Salad	
	Chicken breast	1 pound
	Orzo pasta	1 cup
	Mixed vegetables	To taste
	Tuscan-style Tuna Salad with White Beans	
	Tuna	2 cans
	White beans	1 can
	Greek Tzatziki with Fresh Vegetables	
	Greek yogurt	1 cup
	Cucumber	1
	Fresh vegetables (carrots, celery, bell peppers)	To taste
Day 46		
	Mediterranean Burritos with Tomato and Cheese	

	Burrito wraps	2
	Tomatoes	2
	Cheese	1/2 cup
	Chicken Souvlaki with Greek Salad	
	Chicken breast	1 pound
	Greek salad ingredients (lettuce, tomatoes, cucumber, olives, feta cheese)	To taste
	Baked Mussels with Tomato and Garlic Sauce	
	Mussels	2 pounds
	Tomatoes	4
	Garlic	4 cloves
	Greek-Style Baked Zucchini Chips	
	Zucchini	2
	Bread crumbs	1/2 cup
	Parmesan cheese	1/4 cup
Day 47		
	Overnight Chia Pudding with Quinoa and Berries	
	Chia seeds	1/4 cup
	Quinoa	1/2 cup
	Mixed berries	1 cup
	Roasted Pork Tenderloin with Olives and Capers	
	Pork tenderloin	1 pound
	Olives	1/2 cup
	Capers	2 tablespoons
	Mediterranean-style Fish Tacos	
	Fish fillets (such as cod or tilapia)	1 pound
	Tortillas	8
	Taco fillings (shredded lettuce, diced tomatoes, etc.)	To taste
	Mediterranean Cucumber and Tomato Bites	
	Cucumber	1
	Tomatoes	2
	Feta cheese	1/2 cup
Day 48		
	Whole Grain Tacos with Avocado and Beans	
	Whole grain tortillas	8
	Avocado	2
	Beans (such as black beans or kidney beans)	1 can
	Mediterranean Beef and Vegetable Stir-fry	
	Beef strips	1 pound
	Mixed vegetables	To taste
	Sea Bass with Mediterranean Salsa	
	Sea bass fillets	2
	Salsa ingredients (tomatoes, onions, peppers, etc.)	To taste

	Greek-Style Baked Feta with Honey and Sesame Seeds	
	Feta cheese	8 ounces
	Honey	2 tablespoons
	Sesame seeds	2 tablespoons
Day 49		
	Millet Porridge with Cinnamon Apples	
	Millet	1 cup
	Apples	2
	Cinnamon	1 teaspoon
	Turkey Meatballs with Tomato and Basil Sauce	
	Ground turkey	1 pound
	Tomatoes	2 cans
	Basil	To taste
	Grilled Salmon with Lemon and Dill	
	Salmon fillets	2
	Lemon	1
	Fresh dill	To taste
	Mediterranean Roasted Chickpeas	
	Chickpeas	2 cans
	Olive oil	2 tablespoons
	Seasonings (such as cumin, paprika, garlic powder)	To taste
Day 50		
	Toast with Nut Butter and Banana	
	Whole grain bread	2 slices
	Nut butter (such as peanut butter or almond butter)	2 tablespoons
	Banana	1
	Mediterranean Lamb and Vegetable Skewers	
	Lamb cubes	1 pound
	Mixed vegetables (bell peppers, onions, zucchini, etc.)	To taste
	Mediterranean Shrimp and Vegetable Skewers	
	Shrimp	1 pound
	Mixed vegetables (bell peppers, onions, zucchini, etc.)	To taste
	Chickpea and Olive Bruschetta	
	Chickpeas	1 can
	Olives	1/2 cup
	Baguette	1
Day 51		
	Buckwheat Crepes with Spinach and Feta	
	Buckwheat flour	1 cup
	Spinach	1 cup
	Feta cheese	1/2 cup
	Grilled Pork Chops with Lemon and Oregano	
	Pork chops	2

	Lemon	1
	Oregano	1 teaspoon
	Sea Bass with Mediterranean Salsa	
	Sea bass fillets	2
	Salsa ingredients (tomatoes, onions, peppers, etc.)	To taste
	Chickpea and Olive Bruschetta	
	Chickpeas	1 can
	Olives	1/2 cup
	Baguette	1
Day 52		
	Quinoa Breakfast Bowl with Berries and Nuts	
	Quinoa	1 cup
	Mixed berries	1 cup
	Nuts (such as almonds or walnuts)	1/2 cup
	Chicken Souvlaki with Greek Salad	
	Chicken breast	1 pound
	Greek salad ingredients (lettuce, tomatoes, cucumber, olives, feta cheese)	To taste
	Baked Mussels with Tomato and Garlic Sauce	
	Mussels	2 pounds
	Tomatoes	4
	Garlic	4 cloves
	Greek-Style Baked Zucchini Chips	
	Zucchini	2
	Bread crumbs	1/2 cup
	Parmesan cheese	1/4 cup
Day 53		
	Whole Rye Toast with Avocado and Tomato	
	Whole rye bread	2 slices
	Avocado	1
	Tomato	1
	Chicken Tagine with Olives and Preserved Lemon	
	Chicken thighs	4
	Olives	1 cup
	Preserved lemon	1
	Sardines with Lemon and Olive Oil	
	Sardines	4
	Lemon	1
	Olive oil	2 tablespoons
	Stuffed Grape Leaves (Dolmades)	
	Grape leaves	20
	Rice	1/2 cup
	Fresh herbs (such as parsley, dill)	To taste

Day 54		
	Rye Bread with Smashed Avocado and Poached Egg	
	Rye bread	2 slices
	Avocado	1
	Eggs	2
	Roasted Lamb with Rosemary and Garlic	
	Lamb shoulder	2 pounds
	Rosemary	2 sprigs
	Garlic	6 cloves
	Seafood Risotto with Saffron	
	Mixed seafood (shrimp, scallops, mussels)	1 pound
	Arborio rice	1 cup
	Saffron	1 pinch
	Mediterranean Olive and Feta Skewers	
	Olives	1/2 cup
	Feta cheese	1/2 cup
	Skewers	As needed
Day 55		
	Wheat Berry and Veggie Breakfast Stir-fry	
	Wheat berries	1 cup
	Mixed vegetables	To taste
	Baked Chicken with Artichokes and Capers	
	Chicken pieces (legs, thighs, or breasts)	4
	Artichoke hearts	1 cup
	Capers	2 tablespoons
	Grilled Squid Salad with Lemon and Olive Oil	
	Squid tubes	1 pound
	Lemon	1
	Olive oil	2 tablespoons
	Dates Stuffed with Cheese and Almonds	
	Dates	8
	Cheese (such as goat cheese or cream cheese)	4 ounces
	Almonds	8
Day 56		
	Chia and Quinoa Pudding with Fresh Fruits	
	Chia seeds	1/4 cup
	Quinoa	1/2 cup
	Fresh fruits	To taste
	Chicken Paella with Saffron and Olives	
	Chicken thighs	4
	Saffron threads	1/2 teaspoon
	Olives	1/2 cup
	Baked Trout with Lemon and Thyme	

	Trout fillets	2
	Lemon	1
	Fresh thyme	To taste
	Mediterranean Cucumber and Tomato Bites	
	Cucumber	1
	Tomatoes	2
	Feta cheese	1/2 cup
Day 57		
	Bulgur and Veggie Breakfast Skillet	
	Bulgur	1 cup
	Mixed vegetables	To taste
	Grilled Shrimp with Lemon and Oregano	
	Shrimp	1 pound
	Lemon	1
	Oregano	1 teaspoon
	Quinoa-Stuffed Bell Peppers	
	Bell peppers	4
	Quinoa	1 cup
	Mixed vegetables	To taste
	Greek-Style Baked Zucchini Chips	
	Zucchini	2
	Bread crumbs	1/2 cup
	Parmesan cheese	1/4 cup
Day 58		
	Overnight Oats with Chia and Berries	
	Rolled oats	1 cup
	Chia seeds	2 tablespoons
	Mixed berries	1 cup
	Baked Fish with Lemon and Capers	
	White fish fillets (such as cod or haddock)	2
	Lemon	1
	Capers	2 tablespoons
	Greek-Style Baked Eggplant	
	Eggplant	2
	Tomato sauce	1 cup
	Feta cheese	1/2 cup
	Dates Stuffed with Cheese and Almonds	
	Dates	8
	Cheese (such as goat cheese or cream cheese)	4 ounces
	Almonds	8
Day 59		
	Avocado and Poached Egg Toast	
	Whole grain bread	2 slices

	Avocado	1
	Eggs	2
	Greek Moussaka with Eggplant and Lamb	
	Ground lamb	1 pound
	Eggplant	2
	Tomatoes	2
	Baked Salmon with Lemon and Dill	
	Salmon fillets	2
	Lemon	1
	Fresh dill	To taste
	Greek-Style Yogurt Parfait with Berries and Honey	
	Greek yogurt	1 cup
	Mixed berries	To taste
	Honey	To taste
Day 60		
	Veggie and Whole Grain Breakfast Burrito	
	Whole grain tortillas	2
	Mixed vegetables	To taste
	Greek Salad with Feta and Olives	
	Lettuce	1 head
	Tomatoes	2
	Cucumber	1
	Feta cheese	1/2 cup
	Olives	1/2 cup
	Mediterranean Spaghetti with Garlic and Olive Oil	
	Whole grain spaghetti	8 ounces
	Garlic	4 cloves
	Olive oil	2 tablespoons
	Greek Yogurt with Honey and Pistachios	
	Greek yogurt	1 cup
	Honey	To taste
	Pistachios	To taste

60 DAYS MEAL PLAN

Day	Breakfast	Lunch	Dinner	Snack/Dessert
Day 1	Quinoa Breakfast Bowl with Berries and Nuts	Mediterranean Beef and Vegetable Stir-fry	Grilled Salmon with Lemon and Dill	Greek-Style Hummus with Pita Bread
Day 2	Veggie and Whole Grain Scramble	Beef Tagine with Olives and Preserved Lemon	Greek-style Shrimp with Tomatoes and Feta	Mediterranean Cucumber and Tomato Bites
Day 3	Buckwheat Pancakes with Fresh Berries	Mediterranean Beef Stuffed Bell Peppers	Mediterranean Baked Cod with Olives and Capers	Stuffed Grape Leaves (Dolmades)
Day 4	Whole Rye Toast with Avocado and Tomato	Roasted Pork Tenderloin with Olives and Capers	Seafood Paella with Saffron and Bell Peppers	Mediterranean Olive and Feta Skewers
Day 5	Warm Barley and Berry Breakfast	Grilled Pork Chops with Lemon and Oregano	Tuscan-style Tuna Salad with White Beans	Greek Tzatziki with Fresh Vegetables
Day 6	Chia and Quinoa Pudding with Fresh Fruits	Mediterranean Pork and Bean Stew	Mediterranean Shrimp and Orzo Soup	Greek-Style Baked Feta with Honey and Sesame Seeds
Day 7	Whole Grain Blueberry Muffins	Mediterranean Lamb and Barley Stew	Baked Mussels with Tomato and Garlic Sauce	Chickpea and Olive Bruschetta
Day 8	Millet Porridge with Cinnamon Apples	Roasted Lamb with Rosemary and Garlic	Sea Bass with Mediterranean Salsa	Greek-Style Baked Zucchini Chips
Day 9	Buckwheat Crepes with Spinach and Feta	Greek Lemon Chicken Soup (Avgolemono)	Shrimp and Feta Cheese Orzo	Dates Stuffed with Cheese and Almonds
Day 10	Whole Grain Tacos with Avocado and Beans	Chicken Souvlaki with Greek Salad	Mediterranean-style Fish Tacos	Greek-Style Hummus with Pita Bread
Day 11	Bulgur Wheat Porridge with Raisins and Almonds	Mediterranean Chicken and Vegetable Stir-fry	Grilled Squid Salad with Lemon and Olive Oil	Mediterranean Cucumber and Tomato Bites
Day 12	Toast with Nut Butter and Banana	Chicken Tagine with Olives and Preserved Lemon	Baked Trout with Lemon and Thyme	Stuffed Grape Leaves (Dolmades)
Day 13	Millet and Berry Smoothie Bowl	Mediterranean Chicken and Orzo Salad	Shrimp and Couscous with Feta	Mediterranean Olive and Feta Skewers
Day 14	Apple Cinnamon Whole Grain Pancakes	Chicken Paella with Saffron and Olives	Grilled Scallops with Garlic and Herbs	Greek Tzatziki with Fresh Vegetables
Day 15	Mediterranean Burritos with Tomato and Cheese	Baked Chicken with Artichokes and Capers	Mediterranean Fish Stew with Garlic and Saffron	Greek-Style Baked Feta with Honey and Sesame Seeds

Day	Breakfast	Lunch	Dinner	Snack/Dessert
Day 16	Savory Oatmeal with Sauteed Vegetables	Turkey and Vegetable Stuffed Peppers	Baked Haddock with Olives and Tomatoes	Chickpea and Olive Bruschetta
Day 17	Overnight Chia Pudding with Quinoa and Berries	Mediterranean Turkey and Quinoa Stuffed Eggplant	Grilled Tuna Steaks with Caper Vinaigrette	Mediterranean Roasted Chickpeas
Day 18	Rye Bread with Smashed Avocado and Poached Egg	Turkey Meatballs with Tomato and Basil Sauce	Mediterranean Shrimp and Vegetable Skewers	Dates Stuffed with Cheese and Almonds
Day 19	Greek Yogurt with Honey and Fresh Berries	Grilled Turkey Skewers with Garlic and Herbs	Seafood Risotto with Saffron	Greek-Style Baked Zucchini Chips
Day 20	Mediterranean Fig and Goat Cheese Salad	Greek Lentil Soup (Fakes)	Greek-style Gigantes Plaki (Baked Giant Beans)	Mediterranean Cucumber and Tomato Bites
Day 21	Greek-Style Baked Apples with Honey and Walnuts	Greek Baked Beans with Honey and Dill	Bulgur and Lentil Salad	Stuffed Grape Leaves (Dolmades)
Day 22	Mediterranean Citrus and Olive Salad	Greek-Style Lentil and Spinach Soup	Greek Fava (Yellow Split Pea Puree)	Greek-Style Hummus with Pita Bread
Day 23	Grilled Peach and Mozzarella Salad	Greek-Style Baked Lima Beans (Gigandes)	Buckwheat Salad with Lemon and Olives	Mediterranean Olive and Feta Skewers
Day 24	Mediterranean Pear and Arugula Salad with Feta	Millet Salad with Sun-Dried Tomatoes	Greek-Style Baked Chickpeas with Tomato	Greek Tzatziki with Fresh Vegetables
Day 25	Greek Yogurt Parfait with Fresh Fruits and Honey	Couscous and Lentil Salad	Barley and Chickpea Soup	Greek-Style Baked Feta with Honey and Sesame Seeds
Day 26	Mediterranean Avocado and Strawberry Salad	Greek-Style Black Eyed Peas Salad	Bulgur and Red Lentil Soup	Chickpea and Olive Bruschetta
Day 27	Mediterranean Citrus and Fennel Salad	Greek-Style Brown Rice and Lentil Soup	Quinoa and White Bean Stew	Mediterranean Roasted Chickpeas
Day 28	Mediterranean Apple and Cabbage Slaw	Greek-Style Lentil and Tomato Stew	Quinoa and Cannellini Bean Salad	Dates Stuffed with Cheese and Almonds
Day 29	Greek-Style Cherry Tomato and Watermelon Salad	Greek Chickpea and Spinach Stew	Barley and Lentil Soup with Spinach	Mediterranean Orange and Almond Cake
Day 30	Mediterranean Fruit Salad with Lemon Mint Dressing	Greek Salad with Feta and Olives	Mediterranean Spaghetti with Garlic and Olive Oil	Greek Yogurt with Honey and Pistachios

Day	Breakfast	Lunch	Dinner	Snack/Dessert
Day 31	Millet Porridge with Cinnamon Apples	Chicken Tagine with Olives and Preserved Lemon	Grilled Scallops with Garlic and Herbs	Greek Semolina Pudding with Cinnamon and Raisins
Day 32	Overnight Chia Pudding with Quinoa and Berries	Roasted Pork Tenderloin with Olives and Capers	Quinoa and White Bean Stew	Dates Stuffed with Cheese and Almonds
Day 33	Mediterranean Burritos with Tomato and Cheese	Mediterranean Lamb and Vegetable Skewers	Baked Trout with Lemon and Thyme	Mediterranean Chocolate and Fig Tart
Day 34	Rye Bread with Smashed Avocado and Poached Egg	Turkey Meatballs with Tomato and Basil Sauce	Greek-Style Baked Chickpeas with Tomato	Greek-Style Hummus with Pita Bread
Day 35	Buckwheat Crepes with Spinach and Feta	Chicken Paella with Saffron and Olives	Mediterranean-style Fish Tacos	Lemon and Olive Oil Cake
Day 36	Toast with Nut Butter and Banana	Mediterranean Beef and Vegetable Stir-fry	Greek Lentil Soup (Fakes)	Greek Yogurt with Honey and Pistachios
Day 37	Whole Grain Tacos with Avocado and Beans	Grilled Pork Chops with Lemon and Oregano	Sea Bass with Mediterranean Salsa	Mediterranean Pear and Almond Tart
Day 38	Millet and Berry Smoothie Bowl	Mediterranean Pork and Bean Stew	Shrimp and Couscous with Feta	Mediterranean Orange and Almond Cake
Day 39	Quinoa and Vegetable Breakfast Hash	Beef Tagine with Olives and Preserved Lemon	Greek-Style Lentil and Tomato Stew	Pomegranate and Pistachio Semolina Cake
Day 40	Whole Grain Blueberry Muffins	Mediterranean Chicken and Vegetable Stir-fry	Mediterranean Fish Stew with Garlic and Saffron	Lemon and Rosewater Sorbet
Day 41	Apple Cinnamon Whole Grain Pancakes	Grilled Turkey Skewers with Garlic and Herbs	Greek-Style Lentil and Spinach Soup	Greek Loukoumades (Honey and Cinnamon Doughnuts)
Day 42	Buckwheat Pancakes with Fresh Berries	Mediterranean Lamb and Barley Stew	Baked Haddock with Olives and Tomatoes	Mediterranean Apricot and Almond Tart
Day 43	Warm Barley and Berry Breakfast	Turkey and Vegetable Stuffed Peppers	Barley and Chickpea Soup	Greek-Style Hummus with Pita Bread
Day 44	Veggie and Whole Grain Scramble	Mediterranean Beef Stuffed Bell Peppers	Grilled Tuna Steaks with Caper Vinaigrette	Dates Stuffed with Cheese and Almonds
Day 45	Savory Oatmeal with Sauteed Vegetables	Mediterranean Chicken and Orzo Salad	Tuscan-style Tuna Salad with White Beans	Greek Semolina Pudding with Cinnamon and Raisins

Day	Breakfast	Lunch	Dinner	Snack/Dessert
Day 46	Mediterranean Burritos with Tomato and Cheese	Mediterranean Turkey and Quinoa Stuffed Eggplant	Shrimp and Feta Cheese Orzo	Mediterranean Chocolate and Fig Tart
Day 47	Overnight Chia Pudding with Quinoa and Berries	Roasted Pork Tenderloin with Olives and Capers	Mediterranean-style Fish Tacos	Mediterranean Cucumber and Tomato Bites
Day 48	Whole Grain Tacos with Avocado and Beans	Mediterranean Beef and Vegetable Stir-fry	Sea Bass with Mediterranean Salsa	Greek-Style Baked Feta with Honey and Sesame Seeds
Day 49	Millet Porridge with Cinnamon Apples	Turkey Meatballs with Tomato and Basil Sauce	Grilled Salmon with Lemon and Dill	Mediterranean Roasted Chickpeas
Day 50	Toast with Nut Butter and Banana	Mediterranean Lamb and Vegetable Skewers	Mediterranean Shrimp and Vegetable Skewers	Greek Tzatziki with Fresh Vegetables
Day 51	Buckwheat Crepes with Spinach and Feta	Grilled Pork Chops with Lemon and Oregano	Mediterranean Baked Cod with Olives and Capers	Chickpea and Olive Bruschetta
Day 52	Quinoa Breakfast Bowl with Berries and Nuts	Chicken Souvlaki with Greek Salad	Baked Mussels with Tomato and Garlic Sauce	Greek-Style Baked Zucchini Chips
Day 53	Whole Rye Toast with Avocado and Tomato	Chicken Tagine with Olives and Preserved Lemon	Sardines with Lemon and Olive Oil	Stuffed Grape Leaves (Dolmades)
Day 54	Rye Bread with Smashed Avocado and Poached Egg	Roasted Lamb with Rosemary and Garlic	Seafood Risotto with Saffron	Mediterranean Olive and Feta Skewers
Day 55	Wheat Berry and Veggie Breakfast Stir-fry	Baked Chicken with Artichokes and Capers	Grilled Squid Salad with Lemon and Olive Oil	Dates Stuffed with Cheese and Almonds
Day 56	Chia and Quinoa Pudding with Fresh Fruits	Chicken Paella with Saffron and Olives	Baked Trout with Lemon and Thyme	Mediterranean Cucumber and Tomato Bites
Day 57	Bulgur and Veggie Breakfast Skillet	Grilled Shrimp with Lemon and Oregano	Quinoa-Stuffed Bell Peppers	Greek-Style Baked Zucchini Chips
Day 58	Overnight Oats with Chia and Berries	Baked Fish with Lemon and Capers	Greek-Style Baked Eggplant	Dates Stuffed with Cheese and Almonds
Day 59	Avocado and Poached Egg Toast	Mediterranean Fish and Veggie Grill	Greek-Style Baked Shrimp with Feta	Greek Yogurt with Honey and Walnuts
Day 60	Veggie and Whole Grain Breakfast Burrito	Greek Moussaka with Eggplant and Lamb	Baked Sole with Lemon and Oregano	Greek-Style Yogurt Parfait with Berries and Honey

Printed in Great Britain
by Amazon

24822692R00143